IN CASE YOU WERE
WANDERING

WAYPOINTS FOR TWENTYSOMETHINGS

Travis Miller

In Case You Were Wandering

by Travis Miller

©2012 Travis Miller

Cover Design by Abraham LaVoi, interior layout Tim Cummings

Unless otherwise indicated, all quotations of Scripture are from the New King James Version (NKJV), copyright 1979, 1980, 1982 by Thomas Nelson Inc., Publishers. Some Scripture quotations are from the King James Version (KJV), and some Scripture quotations are from the New International Version (NIV), copyright 1973, 1978, 1984 by International Bible Society.

All rights reserved. No portion of this publication may be reproduced, stored in an electronic system, or transmitted in any form or by any means, electronic, mechanical, photocopy, recording, or otherwise, without the prior permission of Travis Miller. Brief quotations may be used in literary reviews.

Published by

WORD AFLAME PRESS
8855 Dunn Road, Hazelwood, MO 63042
www.pentecostalpublishing.com

Library of Congress Cataloging-in-Publication Data

Miller, Travis, 1964-
  In case you were wandering / by Travis Miller.
      pages cm.
   ISBN 978-1-56722-971-4
1. Self-actualization (Psychology)--Religious aspects--Christianity. 2. Christian life. I. Title.
   BF4598.2.M55 2012
   248.8'4--dc23
                              2012030050

Chelsea and Hayle:

Without you in my life, I'm not sure I would have considered these concepts, rehearsed them in my mind, or shared them with others. Thank you for being who you are and for helping me to be who I am. I am profoundly proud of you. May you never wander.

Contents

Introduction..7
Foreword...9
Chapter One: Explorer or Wanderer?............................11
Chapter Two: What Are My Values? 15
Chapter Three: Discernment and Judgment. 25
Chapter Four: Why Should I Follow God?...................... 33
Chapter Five: Where Is God Leading?............................45
Chapter Six: Who's Going My Direction? 71
Chapter Seven: Ignoring Accountability..........................97
Chapter Eight: Wasting Time. 111
Chapter Nine: Foiled by Frustration. 115
Chapter Ten: Where Do I Go from Here?. 127
Discussion Questions. 137

Introduction

If you picked up this book, then you may be wandering, or know someone who is. Wandering is endemic of young adults, twentysomethings, in contemporary culture. They are expending time, energy, and talent without specific direction. Too many are wandering naturally, spiritually, or both. Rather than consuming such valuable personal resources on adventures leading to nowhere, twentysomethings are better served using those same resources toward achieving a certain life-destination. The intention of these chapters is to help you accomplish that objective. The thoughts and insights offered here are no simple formula, but practical principles. They are offered as waypoints for the journey through this life-stage. Used properly, these waypoints can clarify your destination, provide tools for healthy discovery, and prevent wasting valuable time or talent while wandering aimlessly. Your life is valuable. Your talents are many. Your life is a rich blessing. I pray that these waypoints assist you to realize the wonderful destination that the kingdom of God has prepared for you.

Foreword

It has been said that having potential while one is young is a compliment. However, as you increase in age, it becomes an indictment as it morphs from compliment to curse. Unrealized potential can be tragic and in most instances denotes underachievement, missed opportunities, apathy, and aimlessness. These descriptions could also apply to someone who is wandering. If that's you, then I applaud you for a making a critical step in the right direction by purchasing this book. I truly believe it can be a stabilizing force in your present and foster growth for your future.

While the author, Travis Miller, has been involved with youth ministry in various local and North American capacities, his specialized focus has been on the young adult demographic for quite some time. By virtue of being involved in teaching weekly classes, speaking at special events, contributing to resource production, as well as raising two twentysomethings of his own, his insight and experience pertaining to young adults is vast and real. As a matter of fact, I have had the privilege of gleaning some of the wisdom that you are about to read firsthand.

In Case You Were Wandering is not merely a book to be read in a single sitting and then placed on a bookshelf. It is to be studied, pondered, and applied. A compass is not meant to be consulted once and then put away; rather at needed intervals you review your coordinates and make course corrections to ensure that you stay on the correct path. In the same way, this book is like a guide that will assist you repeatedly in identifying areas where you might be languishing so that you can maneuver your life back on a preferred course.

There are a few books I've come across that I wish I had encountered earlier in my life. Had I done so, there are mistakes I possibly could have avoided, decisions I would have handled differently, and opportunities I would have been prepared to seize. *In Case You Were Wandering* is such a book. Read, relate, and begin to realize the potential resident in you. Let the journey begin!

Shay Mann
General Youth President
United Pentecostal Church International

Chapter One:

Explorer or Wanderer?

"A distressing thing is the obvious aimlessness of the lives of so many people; they are drifting anywhere instead of going somewhere.... And to go just anywhere is the certain way to arrive nowhere."

—William Barclay

Chris McCandless starved to death in an abandoned bus in Denali National Park. Upon discovery, his body weighed sixty-seven pounds. He was twenty-four years old. Just two years prior, he was a bright graduate of Emory University with a promising future. Yet, upon graduation, this son of successful parents left Atlanta without notifying any of his family members. While driving his secondhand Datsun, and eventually hitchhiking, Chris's travels took him across the United States, through many wilderness areas, on his way to Alaska's outback. Chris wasn't on an adventure. Chris was wandering. His aimlessness certainly generated a variety of experiences, yet it ultimately led him to an incredibly senseless and sad ending. In his book *Into the Wild*, Jon Krakauer posits theories for Chris's aimlessness and compares his wandering with

In Case You Were Wandering

other adventurers who met with their demise while roaming. But in the end, one can't interview a dead man. We're not able to know the exact reason for Chris's decisions—only its outcome. Chris's wandering resulted in his untimely demise. His promising life was never fulfilled because he confused discovery with aimlessness.

Aimlessness expends time, energy, and talent without pursuit of specific direction. It leads nowhere. It values experiences above outcomes. It pursues activities without questioning their ultimate purpose or product. Aimlessness loses sight of any destination. Wanderers practice aimlessness, and Chris was a wanderer.

On May 14, 1804, the Corps of Discovery departed Camp Dubois under the direction of Captain William Clark. One week later, the party left Saint Charles, Missouri, having joined with its second leader, Captain Meriwether Lewis. Lewis was twenty-nine years old; Clark, thirty-three. They had been commissioned by President Thomas Jefferson to explore the Louisiana Purchase, to establish trade and US sovereignty over the native peoples along the Missouri River, and to establish a US claim of "Discovery" to the Pacific Northwest. Over the course of their journey they followed the Missouri River to its headwaters, crossed the Continental Divide, canoed the

Chapter One: Explorer or Wanderer?

Clearwater, Snake, and Columbia rivers, and eventually touched foot on the shores of the Pacific Ocean. On March 23, 1806, the Corps of Discovery turned around and headed for home. They arrived in St. Louis on September 23, 1806, after two years, four months, and ten days of exploring. They accomplished their goals of reaching the Pacific and mapping the land to establish a legal presence. They further established trade relations with more than twenty-four indigenous nations. They survived two harsh winters, challenges with some aggressive tribes, and difficulties with terrain and provision. The adventure of the Corps of Discovery was a significant historical accomplishment, perhaps because the group's leaders, Meriwether Lewis and William Clark, embraced discovery yet never lost sight of their ultimate goals.

Discovery is the process of learning, understanding, and mapping one's environment. Discovery has a destination, an end goal that gives the process direction. Discovery enjoys the experiences along the journey, but does so without losing sight of the destination. Explorers practice discovery, and Lewis and Clark were explorers.

Unfortunately, too many aspects of our current culture encourage this generation to get lost in the process and forget about their endpoint. This culture does too much to promote aimlessness and dilute true discovery. We've lost the distinction between wanderers and explorers. In fact, it can be argued this cultural phenomenon has extended the time that twentysomethings spend in the season of discovery. Some young adults are unable to recognize and pursue a life destination and are left wandering aimlessly. Thankfully, not all wanderers meet a sad demise like Chris McCandless; however, too many squander their life's incredible promise. While this is certainly tragic in a natural sense, it becomes starkly shameful in the spiritual sense. The kingdom of God cannot afford to lose the rich, inspiring talents harbored within the lives of this generation.

In response, this book's goal is to assist Christian twentysomethings to embrace the process of life-discovery without getting lost within that same process. Personal growth, understanding distinct strengths and weaknesses, and recognizing individual interests and passions are a natural part of the human life-cycle. Yet, this is just one stage of the life-cycle. This is a process—not a destination within itself. Christians are called to pass through this time of discovery on their way to a God-ordained destination. We are encouraged to recognize and develop the many excellent gifts God has given each of us in a manner that keeps our destination before us. Our discovery should propel us to our ultimate goal. To do so, we must discover our own values and then discern which aspects of discovery enhance those values, and which aspects would instead lead to aimlessness. We are called to be explorers.

Chapter Two:

What Are My Values?

Our busy lives are cluttered with decisions each and every day.
- Should I go out with friends this weekend?
- Should I stay awake a few hours longer surfing the Internet?
- Do I read my Bible today or sleep another half hour?
- Should I skip class today?
- Do I call, text, or email this question?
- Is this the career for me?
- Should I find another job? Quit this one?
- Is this picture fitting to post online?
- Do I go to church or change the oil in my car?
- Should I ask her out for coffee?
- What if he asks me to marry him? Should I?

Life is filled with decisions. Thankfully most decisions we make are not of the life-changing variety when considered individually. Nonetheless, our pattern of decision making and the way we make our choices will definitely set the course for our lives. As you have come to realize, age and maturity allow more empowerment to make our own decisions. And with that power comes the responsibility for our decisions. When we mess up small decisions, the consequences are not usually too bad. But if we mess up big decisions, the outcomes could be disastrous.

- So, is there a process I can follow for making good decisions?
- What makes a decision "good" or "bad"?

Discovery and aimlessness are the result of actions we choose based on our personal values. Ultimately, we say "yes" or "no" to life's various options because of the things we value deep within us. Successful navigation through the sea of discovery is accomplished by individual decisions based on biblical personal values. Yes, we need to know and possess those values, but we also need to weigh each of our decisions against our values. Doing so allows us to stay true to our course and to realize our destination.

But taking the time and energy for this process can be laborious. We have to be thoughtful, intentional. We have to start acting like adults. Of course, we welcome this because we are not children anymore. At the same time, we are not necessarily excited about the extra effort required. So when we allow that laziness to direct us, we skip over thoughtful and intentional decision making to action. Yet, the most immature way to live is to live life as a

Chapter Two: **What Are My Values?**

simple series of actions. Think about it. This is what children do. They go about their days from one action to the next, without any thought whatsoever about the reasons behind their actions.

> Wake up. Eat cereal. Play. Take a nap. Wake up.
> Eat lunch. Play. Take a nap. Wake up again.
> Play some more. Eat dinner. Take a bath. Go to bed.

Children's lives are a series of actions with no personal intention or planning behind them whatsoever. In fact, the actions of children are directed by parents. And the parents are the ones who know the reason behind eating, the purpose of sleeping, the motive for bathing, and so on. Moving from action to action without any thought for the reasons behind the actions is the norm for a child, but it is an immature way to live as an adult.

Typically, as we age, parents begin to explain underlying reasons for actions. That discussion may involve a list of guidelines or rules. After more aging and maturity, we are then informed more about eating, sleeping, and so on. We can understand the biological benefits of sleep—it rejuvenates our cells. We can understand that food gives us energy and even that certain foods are better for our health than other foods. At this more mature level, we can see beyond the actions, and even beyond the guidelines, and into the values behind them. In the end, we eat well and sleep enough because our family values good health. But young adulthood is the time when individuals decide whether or not to possess that same value. Will we value good health? When on our own, will we eat healthy food? Will we get a good night's sleep? Will we consciously adopt these values into our own personal value system? Time will tell.

Of course, the exact same thing is true spiritually. Young adulthood is the time in life that more, and more, and more we are free to make our own choices. We decide for ourselves. Those collective decisions determine aimlessness or discovery.

Here's the problem. Too often, we live spiritually in the most immature way possible. We live like children. We go about our days from one action to the next without ever giving any thought to the reason or intent behind the action. This kind of living is not only spiritually immature, it is also spiritually disastrous. We must be mature enough to recognize that actions are based on personal guidelines, which in turn are derived from personal values. Further, to live as a Christian, our personal values are derived from the nature of God. We discover His nature via the Bible, His Holy Word. The hierarchy looks like this:

Chapter Two: **What Are My Values?**

God:
As known
through Scripture

Values:
The standards of desirability by which
the individual chooses between alternate
behaviors (Merriam Webster Dictionary).

Guidelines:
My process for living out my values.

Actions:
Choosing to live by all the above.

Here's where the big transition takes place for young adults. It is at this age, during this life-stage, that we transition from external guidelines and values to internal guidelines and values. When we were children in our homes, we depended on parents to set the guidelines. We depended on them to know the values and to understand how to apply them to guidelines and ultimately, actions. In the classroom we depended upon teachers to know values and to establish guidelines. In the church, we depended on spiritual leadership for those values and guidelines. Since we were children, we did not need to bother with any of that. Our lives were a series of actions under the direction of the adults who were responsible for our lives.

Not anymore.

Independence is great. But I cannot just walk away from the guidelines and values of the important adults in my life. I must establish my own. I must adopt and rely upon values and guidelines that I will use to make my decisions, to guide my actions, to live my life.

For instance, in our society today, marriage continues to be devalued. Not only does our culture ignore biblical instruction on marriage, but it also ignores the proven societal, financial, and familial benefits of marriage. Fewer twentysomethings are getting married, and of those who do, few expect to be married to that person for the rest of their lives. But what about you? What do you believe about marriage? What are your values concerning marriage? Ultimately, your marriage values will determine whom you date, whom you enter into a relationship with, whether or not

Chapter Two: **What Are My Values?**

you'll offer or accept a marriage proposal, and the commitment you will take into it. Your individual actions regarding marriage will depend on your individual values for the institution.

Certainly we have the benefit of seeking counsel from loving parents, and we have the benefit of God-fearing pastors and other valuable mentors. However, as adults, it is now our responsibility to establish our own guidelines, to personally discover the values behind those guidelines, and finally to determine in our own hearts that we will base those values on the nature of almighty God. Those who do not take this responsibility, and make this transition, are certain to battle ongoing challenges, and are not likely to succeed as Christians. In fact, those who live life without any consideration of why decisions are made or actions are taken are quite likely to be wanderers.

WAYPOINT: ▶ **Values are invaluable.**

Business leader Steven Covey wrote, "The ability to subordinate an impulse to a value is the essence of the proactive person. Reactive people are driven by feelings, by circumstances, by conditions, by their environment. Proactive people are driven by values—carefully thought about, selected, and internalized values." Combining Covey's thoughts with the previous descriptions, we recognize that reactive people end up wandering and proactive people end up at their destination. Proactive people have an understanding of the value of values, which then functions as predetermined direction.

Perhaps we can recognize the importance more clearly when we compare our actions, guidelines, and values to the operation of an automobile. Decisions are like the steering wheel. At every intersection, we decide whether to proceed right, left, or straight ahead. Drivers may never lose control of their automobiles, yet still end up totally lost, or somewhere they never intended to be. Personal values are comparable to a GPS device. By using a GPS, the driver can plot his course to an intended destination. Then, as the car approaches an intersection, the decision to turn or go forward is dictated by the GPS unit as it directs toward the entered endpoint. Actually, values encompass even more than the role of the GPS unit. Yes, the GPS helps determine our course,

Chapter Two: What Are My Values?

but we still have to enter the proper destination. Used to their fullest, values dictate our direction and our destination. Our values determine individual choices at life's intersections, but they also determine our final destination.

The error many make is to base their guidelines and decisions on their current location. Decisions based solely on our current situation lead to random destinations. Wandering. When life is just a series of actions not based on values, we are left vulnerable to feelings, circumstances, environment, culture, and so on. Can you imagine the car ride that doesn't consider any destination? Can you imagine the driver who muses, "We'll just figure this out as we go. At each intersection we'll decide whether to turn right or left, go straight, or turn around. Then we'll just see where it takes us"? Exciting? Maybe. Adventurous? Perhaps. Enjoyable? Possibly. But this is a driver who has lost sight of a particular destination. All emphasis is placed on the joy in the journey without regard to an endpoint. Where will the driver be when his journey is complete? Who knows? Random decisions lead to random destinations.

Now, before you get too offended, this is not to propose an "either-or" situation, but instead recommend a "both-and" scenario. We can make value-based decisions and enjoy the journey en route. We can, and should, be excited about the adventure we experience on our way to our ultimate destination.

In Case You Were Wandering

However, we have to be very careful not to get so enamored with the trip that we forget where we intended to go. Values are waypoints that allow us to be explorers rather than wanderers.

Values help us make our choices and establish our destination. But there are times when the correct choice is not too clear. Life brings us to intersections we've not encountered previously with more options than right or left. For these times, we look to the waypoint known as discernment.

Chapter Three:

Discernment and Judgment

Have you ever been following a GPS device in your car and when it instructed you to make a turn, there was no road to turn onto? Have you had the device tell you to make a turn, after you've already exited the intersection? Or have you experienced a time when the map displayed on the GPS just didn't match the area where you were? When the GPS is giving clear directions in a timely fashion, that match the terrain, it is really quite easy to continue on the route. All systems are "go." But sometimes, the GPS just does not readily describe our situation.

As we make our way through life, doing our best to follow our chosen path, listening as best we can to our God-mapped values, there are times when those values do not easily hold us on course. Sometimes our situation does not fit neatly into our value map. Or perhaps our values cannot be heard as clearly because of all the life-noise around us. In times like these, being able to follow

In Case You Were Wandering

our values requires more attention and energy. We might have to slow down; we might even have to stop. We may need to look around some. Need to ask some questions of those nearby. Need to take our lives off of autopilot and discern our circumstance more carefully. We have to consider all aspects of our situation, discover what personal values apply to the situation, and make a judgment on how we will apply our values in order to move forward.

Some years ago I read a story about Pepperdine University student Brian Bushway. The article spoke of Brian's mountain biking abilities, though he could not drive a car, nor recognize colors. At the age of fourteen, optic nerve atrophy left Brian completely blind. However, later he met Dan Kish, an expert in echolocation. Echolocation is a navigational technique used by people to perceive objects through the reflection of sound waves. Kish, himself blind since birth, taught Brian to click his tongue and listen to the sound reverberation created. Using the echoes, Brian is able to recognize everything from a piece of Plexiglas to a playing card. Today, Bushway and others trained by Kish are able to use echolocation to bicycle trails as well as dirt roads. The article quoted Bushway as saying, "This

Chapter Three: Discernment and Judgment

isn't amazing or impossible." I cannot imagine riding a bicycle blind. However, Brian can say it is not amazing because he has trained his sense of hearing to discern between various echoes. He has honed his ability to discern.

Discernment is the process of information gathering and assessment that prepares us for a decision. We use our senses, our minds, and any other reliable sources of information to determine our surroundings and circumstances. We look around, check the map, and search for landmarks. Discernment is an acquired skill that is perfected through practice. The Bible teaches that mature Christians should have their senses exercised to discern both good and evil (Hebrews 5:14). As highlighted by Brian's and Dan's lives, it is truly amazing how sharp our discernment senses can be when we exercise them. We too have to exercise our ability to discern the various aspects of our circumstances in order to judge between good and evil and make the right decisions.

In Case You Were Wandering

WAYPOINT: **Some people struggle with judgment.**

To make a judgment, we have to make a choice between good and better, between better and best, or sometimes between good and bad. When we do this, when we choose one thing over another, often there is another person we know who chose the option that we disregarded. And when that person is someone close to us, someone familiar with our choice, we might be labeled as "judgmental." When I select option A over option B, and my friend selects option B over option A, my friend might think my choice for my life-course is also a negative judgment of their decision. Thus, a personal decision to harmonize God-mapped values with my life-path has now become a relational issue. In some cases, my friend becomes offended by my choice and will respond by labeling me "judgmental." In his opinion, I am issuing judgment on his life, but in reality I am just using judgment to guide my own life.

Labeling Christians "judgmental" is immensely popular in current culture, which any reasonable person has to find ironic. Usually, the ones who are quick to do so know just enough Scripture to be dangerous. They will quickly quote "Judge not, that you be not judged" (Matthew 7:1). When anyone chooses to label anyone else "judgmental" they are making a judgment themselves! In truth, what such a person is saying is, "It is OK for me to judge you, but not for you to judge me." Convenient.

If those who are so quick to quote the first verse of Matthew chapter 7 would take the time to read further in the chapter, they would find that judgment is a necessary skill to pursue Christianity. In fact, judgment is necessary to follow any set of life-values. Any who would follow a chosen belief system must make personal judgments in light of that system, or they are not staying true to their stated beliefs.

Yes, within the first five verses of Matthew 7, Jesus teaches that we are not to cast judgment upon others without making consideration for our own faults. However, that is not the end of the judgment subject. Judgment is more nuanced than that. Notice in verse 6 of that same chapter Jesus said, "Do not give what is holy to the dogs; nor cast your pearls before swine, lest they trample them under their feet, and turn and tear you in pieces." Jesus instructs us that holy things and pearls should not be given to dogs and swine. Defining something as holy, or as a pearl, requires making a judgment. Further, how can we recognize a dog or a pig unless we make a judgment? Later in the same chapter Jesus said this:

In Case You Were Wandering

"Beware of false prophets, who come to you in sheep's clothing, but inwardly they are ravenous wolves. You will know them by their fruits. Do men gather grapes from thornbushes or figs from thistles? Even so, every good tree bears good fruit, but a bad tree bears bad fruit. A good tree cannot bear bad fruit, nor can a bad tree bear good fruit. Every tree that does not bear good fruit is cut down and thrown into the fire. Therefore by their fruits you will know them" (Matthew 7:15-20).

By their fruits we determine good trees from bad. Whether a tree, or a situation, or a person is good or bad is determined by its fruit, or its outcomes, or his actions. Matching outcomes to labels requires a judgment on our part—a judgment taught and encouraged by Jesus Himself. Therefore if we are fooled by popular culture's faulty reasoning, and even some within Christian circles, then we are not taking into account the fullness of Jesus' teaching on judgment. Rather, we are selecting the portions of His teaching that suit our preferences and ignoring those that do not; a sure way to misconstrue Scripture, and to end up wandering.

Chapter Three: Discernment and Judgment

Instead of wandering, explorers balance their thinking. No, we are not to judge others while excusing our own faults. However, in order to follow the Lord's commandments and instructions, to remain true to our God-mapped values, we have to make some judgments. We must discern between good and better, between better and best, and between good and bad. It is purely a matter of staying on course.

And yet, having such insight and understanding, we continue to face obstacles on our path of discovery. In fact, one of those obstacles is our own ignorance. Though diligent in our pursuit of knowledge and understanding, there is no way that we can know all things. There is so much to know. Only God is omniscient. As the prophet recognized, "O Lord, I know the way of man is not in himself; It is not in man who walks to direct his own steps" (Jeremiah 10:23).

No man, none of us, has all the answers we need to direct our paths. We can use discernment and judgment to make choices in alignment with our personal values. But if our personal values are only values created and fostered by mankind, then we are following faulty values. A wrong destination has been entered into our personal GPS.

In Case You Were Wandering

Christians do not use these principles to arrive at merely temporal destinations. We cannot depend on ordinary human understanding to enter our life's coordinates. It must be Jesus Christ who enters the coordinates into our personal GPS. He has to be the one who sets our direction.

But, where is God leading?

Chapter Four:

Why Should I Follow God?

They had not seen the sun or stars for days. They had not eaten for a long time. They had thrown overboard most everything not tied down. In fact, they had given up hope of being rescued.

Then Paul called the shipmates together for a small-group meeting. He opened the session by reminding everyone that this situation would not have happened had they listened to him: an old-fashioned "I-told-you-so." Human nature even got the best of Paul on occasion. Yet he went on to declare they would lose the ship and be shipwrecked on an island for a while, but in the end, no one would lose their lives.

And how did he know this? Paul had experienced an angelic visitation. In fact, he said that "it was an angel of the God to whom I belong and whom I serve." He then went on to declare his conviction that "it will be just as it was told me" (Acts 27:23-25).

WAYPOINT: **I belong to God.**

Though it is interesting that Paul possessed such faith in God in the middle of dire circumstances, it is more intriguing to learn how he possessed this faith. What brought him to this place of faith in the face of extraordinary circumstances? How could he be so confident when he had witnessed nothing but storm clouds for days on end?

The answer rests in the few words Paul used to describe his angelic visit. He said it was an angel of "the God to whom I belong." In fact, it could very well be that these words signify the foundation for his later comment: "I believe God that it will be just as it was told me." Paul seems to have placed great faith in the words of his God that stemmed from this understanding of belonging.

Indeed Paul's assurance in the Lord proved legitimate. Following more than fourteen days at sea, the crew was shipwrecked. Yet no lives were lost. They spent many months on the island of Malta, but in time they left to continue their trip. And all of these happened just as was foretold by the angel of the Lord.

Chapter Four: **Why Should I Follow God?**

Of course, Paul was not surprised in the least by this outcome. He knew that God would perform as promised because Paul belonged to Him.

WAYPOINT: **I'm God's possession.**

Just what does belonging to God mean? For many, belonging most obviously speaks of possession: to be the property of a person or thing. Paul explained to the Corinthians, "Do you not know that your body is the temple of the Holy Spirit who is in you, whom you have from God, and you are not your own? For you were bought at a price; therefore glorify God in your body and in your spirit, which are God's" (I Corinthians 6:19-20). Having entered into the kingdom of God through biblical salvation, as Christians we are not our own; we belong to God. Though it may be something we have heard a number of times and in various settings, it is still good to be reminded that we were bought with a price. (See also Hebrews 9:12-15.)

Calvary purchased our salvation. Christ's death, burial, and resurrection paid for our cleansing. His shed blood obtained individual opportunity to repent of sins, the chance to be baptized in His name, and the prospect of being filled with His Spirit. Or in the words of Peter, "Knowing that you were not redeemed with corruptible things, like silver or gold... but with the precious blood of Christ, as of a lamb without blemish and without spot" (I Peter 1:18-19). As such, we belong to God. We are not our own. In terms of possession, He is the God to whom we belong.

> **WAYPOINT:** I am an heir to God's kingdom.

Belonging fittingly refers to possession, but it is not limited to that concept. When we belong to God, there are other implications for our lives. Belonging speaks of participation: to be attached or bound by birth, allegiance, or dependency.

In belonging to God, we are bound to Him by birth. We are not His simply through friendship or acquaintance, but we have been born into His family. Jesus instructed, "Most assuredly, I say to you, unless one is born of water and the Spirit, he cannot enter the kingdom of God. That which is born of the flesh is flesh, and that which is born of the Spirit is spirit" (John 3:5-6).

Chapter Four: Why Should I Follow God?

Paul addresses the same concept when writing to the church at Rome. "For as many as are led by the Spirit of God, these are sons of God. For you did not receive the spirit of bondage again to fear, but you received the Spirit of adoption by whom we cry out, 'Abba, Father'" (Romans 8:14-15). Christians are not strangers, not outcasts, nor outsiders. But by the infilling of the Holy Ghost, we are sons. We belong to Him because we were born into His kingdom by the Holy Ghost.

Additionally, this belonging goes beyond birth and proceeds toward allegiance. Obviously, every child can point to the existence of a father. All can recognize one who gave them life. But it is another thing to offer one's allegiance. "The God to whom I belong" refers to the One to whom I am loyal. Christians recognize the blessing He has given us; therefore we are devoted to Him. Thus, belonging to Him is more than mere acknowledgement of His existence, but we have become faithful to Him. Whether feast or famine, good times or bad, blessing or cursing, we belong to Him. Our allegiance is with Him.

In Case You Were Wandering

WAYPOINT: **I enjoy a relationship with God.**

Probably the most wonderful understanding of belonging is that of a close relationship. This speaks of the unique and blessed belonging that is found in family—the belonging expressed between parents and children or grandparents and their grandchildren. It is the wondrous sense of belonging that exists between husband and wife. This dimension of belonging is based on relationship. Not simply the blood relationship, but relationship founded on an understanding of the other.

In such relationships, we belong because we are loved. We belong because we are accepted. We are supported and comforted. As a result of times of sharing and conversation we sense that belonging. Since we have stood by one another in difficult times, we are certain we belong. So it is with our God: the God to whom we belong.

Chapter Four: Why Should I Follow God?

WAYPOINT: **I am in the right place.**

In belonging to God, we have an understanding that we are properly classified, that we are in a proper situation. We have the right label. We have been given the correct name. We are as those referenced in the Book of Acts "who belonged to the Way" (Acts 9:2, NIV). Or possibly we might better relate to the words recorded in Isaiah: "One will say, 'I belong to the LORD'; another will call himself by the name of Jacob; still another will write on his hand, 'The LORD's,' and will take the name Israel" (Isaiah 44:5, NIV).

We belong to the Lord. In Him we are Christians, believers, children of the King, the redeemed, and saints of the Most High. Saints ought to rightly recognize that belonging to Him is proper recognition. It is a logo to wear well. It is a name to carry proudly, an association with which to be incredibly comfortable. This is where we fit in. We have found our place.

In Case You Were Wandering

WAYPOINT: **Every promise in the Book is mine.**

In belonging to God and His kingdom, we become a part, an extension, of something much bigger than ourselves. Within that extension, we enjoy the promises and perks of that bigger entity. For instance, as a member of the American Automobile Association (AAA), I receive the benefits of membership. Free towing, roadside assistance, travel planning, and other advantages are all accessible to me because I belong to an organization bigger than myself.

When I belong to the Lord, there are also perks, privileges, and promises that are mine. Paul said, "If you belong to Christ, then you are Abraham's seed, and heirs according to the promise" (Galatians 3:29, NIV). Peter wrote, "Nevertheless we, according to His promise, look for new heavens and a new earth in which righteousness dwells" (II Peter 3:13). And John penned, "This is the promise that He has promised us—eternal life" (I John 2:25). Or, as the old songwriter composed, "Every promise in the Book is mine, every chapter, every verse, every line."

Chapter Four: Why Should I Follow God?

When we belong to Christ, there is an inheritance of blessing that is simply a part of the package.

This aspect of belonging is especially good to recall in the midst of a culture that can be so critical of Christianity. I recall a time as a twentysomething when I was not as versed in this aspect of belonging. On one particular weekend, I was helping a traveling construction crew finish painting a water tower. Over lunch one day, the foreman of the job noted my Christianity and proceeded to share with me, and everyone at the table, his views of the same. In his mind, the kingdom of God, with all of its "trappings," was no more than a crutch. To him Christianity was only for those who could not successfully navigate their own lives. His unspoken implication was that since he did not have any addictions, tragedies, or relationship problems in his life, then he had no need for Christ. Unfortunately, he caught me without a reasonable answer. So I just sat there, staring at my lunch plate.

Thankfully, since that time I have come to realize that belonging to God means so much more than assistance with life's difficulties. Again, consider AAA. As a member for many years, I have found that there are a number of good reasons to belong to this organization. Most regard AAA as the group that can start your car when the battery is dead, send a locksmith when you have locked the keys in the car, or tow the car when you have landed in a ditch on a snowy day. However, there are other privileges of membership besides just being rescued from trouble. Members receive 30 percent discounts on eyeglasses and exams for the entire family. There are discounts on purchases at some popular stores. When going on a trip, we obtain numerous travel-planning perks. In fact, I do not ever have to need a tow truck to appreciate my membership. I have come to see AAA for all that it really is. In addition to its hazard benefits, it is loaded with privileges.

And the same is true for the kingdom of God. What a blessing it is for Christians to recognize and declare that belonging to God is not just a rescue operation. Certainly God delivers addicts, mends relationships, cures diseases, and cleanses mankind from sin. However, He is not solely about deliverance. There are blessings, promises, and spiritual perks that are a wonderful part of being a member. I enjoy the encouragement, accountability and camaraderie of fellow Christians. I am impacted with valuable life-lessons from spiritual leaders. I am privileged to participate in corporate worship with my local assembly. And the list can go on and on. Since I belong to Christ, my life can be filled with these blessings and so many more. Membership has its privileges.

Chapter Four: Why Should I Follow God?

WAYPOINT: **So I believe God.**

A final benefit of belonging to God is a matter of faith. When Paul spoke to the men in that storm-ravaged ship, he ended his discourse by noting "I believe God that it will be just as it was told me" (Acts 27:25). When we are possessed by a heartfelt understanding of our belonging to God, then we have the awesome benefit of genuine confidence in Him. While in the midst of turmoil or difficulty, we are not swayed or dismayed, but rather we can stand strong on the promises we have received of our Lord. We can speak with the confidence of Paul and declare: I believe God that it will be just as it was told me. Why? Because I belong to God.

Chapter Five:

Where Is God Leading?

Late in my Bible College career, we had the privilege of a missionary visiting our campus. After speaking to the student body and lecturing in some classes, he took a chair in one of the staff offices and opened the door for any student to stop by and speak with him. I'd never had the chance to speak to a missionary in such a one-on-one situation, so I jumped at the chance. When I got to the hallway near the office, there was a line of students waiting for their turn. While standing in that line, I decided to ask questions like: How can I determine God's direction for my life? What am I going to do once I graduate from here?

Missionary Robert Rodenbush's reply went something like this:

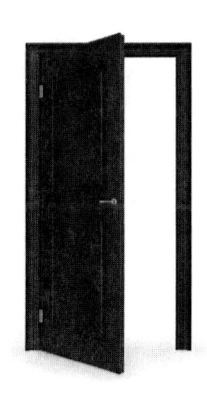

> "Suppose I was in a room with a couch and a number of doors. Imagine that those doors represent the things that I could do with my life; that behind one of those doors

> was God's will for my life. Now, there are many people who would sit on that couch, and begin to heartily pray that God would open the door He wants them to go through. But not me. I would walk around that room and try each doorknob to see what doors will open. My prayer would be 'Lord, if this door is not for me, then keep it locked. Otherwise, I'm going through open doors.'"

Obviously, that parable has stayed with me. And I share it because it represents some different perspectives on pursuing God's calling on our lives. It reflects different ways of answering the question, "Where is God leading?"

Any consideration regarding the pursuit of God's direction needs to begin with a very clear statement: If you are willing for God to use you, He is willing to put you to work. There is definitely something for you to do in the kingdom of God. According to researchers, world population has now eclipsed seven billion. Until each of them has heard about Jesus and been given an opportunity to find Bible salvation, there is plenty of work to be done. As long as there are disciples to be made, there is work for all of us to do.

Chapter Five: **Where Is God Leading?**

Yet I imagine that knowing and believing these statements still doesn't bring absolution to our personal questions. Questions like:

- "I know that there is plenty of work to be done, but what work am I to do?"
- "What's my calling?"
- "What direction should I be going?"

These questions can be problematic. For instance, we make the assumption that there is just one perfect thing that I ought to be doing for God. For many of us, the issue is not that we don't have anything to do with our lives. Instead, the issue is that we have so many things we could do with our lives. We are blessed with multiple opportunities. Unfortunately, this blessing can also be a curse. It's possible to be crippled by too many choices.

WAYPOINT: **Understand that our calling does not need to be limited to just one thing.**

I graduated from Bible college in 1987—a long time ago. At that time there were not a bunch of ministry specialties. We had some classes in music, some classes directed toward Christian education, a few classes on public speaking, and then many doctrine classes. We studied the Word of God and were challenged to pursue the work of God. All of it. Do anything and everything you can.

Today, there are many more specialties.

Students involved in music ministry, or children's ministry follow much more focused coursework than in my day. And there are many more focused ministries from which to choose. In my day, we simply had a speech class. And in that class, we tried to preach. Today, ministerial students enjoy a variety of specialized preaching classes with emphasis on different manners of presentation, different audiences, and much more. All of this is wonderful. It's thrilling that students can receive such specialized training. However, there is a downside also, and that is the feeling that students have to choose just one thing to pursue.

- Should I be an evangelist or a pastor?
- Should I be a music minister or pursue children's ministry?
- Should I be a youth pastor or outreach director?

Why do any of these have to be either/or? How about both/and? There are many things that we can be involved in for the kingdom of God! When searching for God's direction for our lives,

Chapter Five: **Where Is God Leading?**

understand that our calling does not need to be limited to just one thing.

This same truth applies to secular education and careers. A few decades ago, college students pursued general areas of study related to a handful of areas such as education, engineering, health care, or law. Over the years, these general classifications have been diversified into numerous specialties within each discipline. As with ministry, the numerous options can be debilitating for some students. Our assumption is that we need to choose just one thing to pursue. With such a large variety of options, the decision can seem too daunting.

At times, students can be overwhelmed like the child who visits the large candy store at the mall. The entire store is filled with every kind of candy that a child can imagine, and many that they haven't—candy of all sizes, shapes, colors, and flavors. Given the opportunity by her grandpa to choose two or three candies from the hundreds of selections, she might not know where to start. She could immediately choose a couple of candies that she's tasted previously, but if she does, then she does not get the chance to taste some new ones that catch her eye. As she peruses the store, she picks up and puts down many different candies. After a while, she becomes saddened and frustrated when confronted with the choice. There are just too many candies that she really would like to try. Having to narrow her choice down to two or three seems almost impossible. What should have been an incredibly exciting opportunity has turned into a frustrating situation due to all of the options available. All the while, this same child could have easily chosen a candy if that same loving grandfather had presented just two options, one in his right hand and the other in his left. Choose one or the other. She could have more readily handled the choice if the options were greatly reduced. At times, students approach college majors and career choices in a similar fashion. If the choices are limited, fine; but if there are multiple opportunities, frustration seems likely.

While removing options can make the decision easier, it also limits opportunities, which doesn't seem beneficial. As knowledge continues to rapidly increase in our world, the need for specialties is not going away. Rather, the trend to have numerous choices for specializing will probably continue. Therefore, students should ease their personal tension by understanding some general things about God's direction in their lives.

Chapter Five: Where Is God Leading?

WAYPOINT: **Hyper-Spiritual or Plainly Pragmatic?**

Another challenge we face when pursuing God's direction is that too often Christians regard the hyper-spiritual above the plainly pragmatic. Sometime back I listened to the story of a church planter who told me how God clearly and certainly spoke to him. He heard from God on a specific corner sidewalk in the city he was to plant a church. He told me that many times when he was feeling defeated, tired, or doubtful, he would return to that very corner and talk to the Lord. He would stand on that sidewalk and be reminded again of God's promise to him. Certainly this is a powerfully spiritual experience. And I believe every word.

On the other hand, I have listened to global missionaries who planted churches under much different circumstances. The missionary recognized a city nearby that didn't have a Christian church. So the missionary started going into that city to preach. Then he started taking another couple along on these visits. In time, this couple could be trained to pastor this new church. And they just kept going back, and kept preaching, and kept training until there was a church in that city with a pastoral family. There is no mention of a powerful, unique move of God on that missionary before stepping out to start the church. He just had the pragmatic realization that there was a city that didn't have a church. So he went to start one. And did.

Of these two stories, which one sounds the most dramatic, exciting, and spiritual? Which one are we more likely to hear exemplified in sermons? Which story is more likely to be reported about in denominational newsletters or magazines? We are probably more likely to hear about the dramatic story of God speaking to the preacher on the city street corner. But the global missionary also heard from God. He simply heard God's voice in a more pragmatic way. He humbly read the words of Jesus in Matthew and followed them.

"And Jesus came and spoke to them, saying, 'All authority has been given to Me in heaven and on earth. Go therefore and make disciples of all the nations, baptizing them in the name of the Father and of the Son and of the Holy Spirit, teaching them to observe all things that I have commanded you; and lo, I am with you always, even to the end of the age.' Amen" (Matthew 28:18-20).

As we seek for God to order our steps, we must understand that our calling doesn't need to be hyper-spiritual, nor does it need to be plainly pragmatic. It is likely to fall somewhere in between, involve a little portion of both, and be unique to each of us. To help us find where God is going, the balance of this chapter offers some pragmatic understanding.

Chapter Five: **Where Is God Leading?**

WAYPOINT: **Understand what the Bible says.**

Did you know that 97.6 percent of God's will is found in the Word of God? As the psalmist wrote, "Your word is a lamp to my feet and a light to my path" (Psalm 119:105). The "lamp to my feet" represents that which is near, close, or soon to happen. In contrast, the "light to my path" is associated with things that are farther away, at a distance, or occurring later. And neither of these phrases leads us to believe that the path is illuminated as far as the eye can see. Instead, the unknown is invariably involved. We are not going to know 100 percent of God's plan for our future. And if we did, then how would faith fit into the picture? After all, Paul told the Corinthians that we walk by faith, not by sight (II Corinthians 5:7).

When it comes to finding God's direction for our lives, here is another essential statement to remember: Just because we don't know everything, doesn't mean that we don't know anything. This truth is important because our perspective affects our actions. We can stand still and fret over the little bit that we don't know, or we can keep walking based on all the things that we do know. We can look off into that future darkness and remain at a fearful standstill in life, or we can continue to walk in the light that we have. If we choose to remain motionless for the fear of the unknown, then we'll not realize the benefits of all that is clearly known. But if we'll accept the fact that we don't need to know everything in order to know something, then we can use all of the knowledge and light that God has provided us for this time. Pragmatically speaking, God's Word holds an overwhelming majority of the illumination that we need.

Here's the thing: having that light is not always as easy as switching on the button of a flashlight. Illumination is usually revealed with varying degrees of effort. In some instances, the light that we need is given to us in a simple verse or few verses of Scripture that directly and specifically address our circumstance. As a cycling aficionado I often recognize the bicycles others are riding. Prior to one group ride, I noticed a cyclist preparing his bike for the tour. It was a Pinarello Prince, a beautiful bike valued at more than $10,000.00. I would really like to own such a bike. Italian made. Carbon fiber. Pristine paint job. But I don't have that kind of cash to spend on a bike. So, I could have stolen it from him. That was an option available to me as I envied his bicycle. Of course, that would clearly be outside of God's direction because the Scripture plainly declares, "You shall not steal" (Exodus 20:15). That simple verse

Chapter Five: Where Is God Leading?

directly addressed my circumstance. The light of God's direction was simple and clear.

But at other times, there doesn't seem to be a straightforward verse that addresses my need, or the application of the verse is not straightforward. On those occasions, we have to rely on the principles that are established in God's Word: principles of righteousness, self-control, goodness, compassion, and so on. This is more difficult. Applying God's principles to our specific situations requires more work. I might know certainly that God wants me to be compassionate to my neighbor, but exactly how am I to show that compassion? If my friend is out of work and doesn't have money for groceries, then compassion would tell me to buy him some food. But if he remains out of work for a long time and does not seem to be looking for a job, how long should I keep buying his groceries? At some time along the way would I be more compassionate to help him look for a job? Help him fill out applications and prepare for interviews? Applying God's principles to our specific situations is labor intensive. It takes time. It requires plenty of prayerful consideration. It's not easy and it's not quick. But it's what we must do when we want God's illumination for our life's path.

The problem is that human nature prefers easy answers to those that involve hard work. We prefer the path of least resistance. It's the reason we like professors to provide study guides prior to exams. It's the reason we use the Internet to find book summaries rather than actually read the book. There is this ongoing voice in our head that posits, "There must be an easier way!" That leads to some difficult questions:

- When I am praying and asking God for direction, am I doing so because I don't want to do the hard work of finding, understanding, and applying His scriptural principles to my life?
- Am I praying and hoping that God will give me an answer so that I don't have to discover it?
- Do I want God to give me an answer because that would be easier?

Maybe God's response to our prayer is simple. Maybe He is personalizing the psalmist. "My word is a lamp to your feet and a light to your path." After all, 97.6 percent of God's direction is found in the Word of God.

And, in case you're wondering how the 97.6 percent figure was derived, it's simple. No surveys, no social research, no mathematical calculations. I just chose the number to catch your attention and to summarize the point that nearly all that we need to know about finding God's direction is located in the principles and directives of His Holy Word.

> **WAYPOINT:** **Understand that God seems to be consistent in how He speaks to individuals.**

Though not a scientific survey, I've polled quite a few ministers and long-time Christians on this point: Does God speak to you in a variety of ways, or does He seem to be consistent in His method of communicating with you? Most of the time, folks find God to be consistent. This doesn't mean that He talks to you and me in the same fashion. We might hear Him in a still, small voice; by a strong impression in our spirit; through a dream; or via our thoughts. The different manners suggest that God speaks to individuals in varying ways. However, He's usually consistent in the method He uses with an individual. I am suggesting that the way He has been talking to you up to this point is likely to be the manner He'll speak to you going forward. Maybe He'll decide to direct you in a new and unusual way. After all He is God and He can do as he wishes.

However, time has shown that He's usually consistent in His dealings with individuals.

> **WAYPOINT:** **Understand who you are.**

In addition to the personal values that we addressed in Chapter Two, it is further important to recognize individual abilities and interests. What do I like? What am I good at? What things do I volunteer for? What are my strengths and weaknesses? If I like children, and I'm good with children, then there is a very real possibility that one avenue in which I can serve God is in children's ministry. If I am great with English, and my writing gets my friends' and family's attention, then it could be that one area of my ministry will be through the written word. If I am confident with people I've just met, and comfortable speaking in different settings and with small groups, then I might be the perfect person to teach Bible studies in my city. Relating my interests and abilities to God's opportunities can help to locate His direction for me.

If you still are unclear of your strengths or interests, a personality test can help you find your natural bent and abilities.

Chapter Five: Where Is God Leading?

There are a number of popular tests available (MBTI, True Colors, and others) that offer descriptions of your personality and practical applications for your preferences. For some, a personality test can bring about genuine insight.

While in high school my youngest daughter was working part time in a fast food restaurant. She hated it. From nearly the first day, she despised going to work. Though my wife and I continued to encourage her and offer suggestions, she remained distraught. Of course, she often spoke of quitting the job, but we encouraged her to keep the job until she found another. Near the peak of her frustration, she took the Myers-Briggs Type Indicator (MBTI) at school. I'll never forget the day she received the report from this test. The results included a listing of the top ten jobs people of her personality type are most likely to enjoy and also the top ten jobs they are likely to dislike. She waved the report in our faces while highlighting the most disliked job for her personality type: fast food employee. Now she had scientific proof to quit the job she despised. Yes, a personality test can increase understanding of who we are.

However, there is a double-edged sword to understanding who I am: Understanding who I am should not excuse me from meeting a need or growing as a Christian. I must not limit God to just the abilities and interests that I currently possess. Understanding who

In Case You Were Wandering

I am is a necessary aspect of this discovery; however, it's not the entire discovery. In addition to understanding myself, I should also:

WAYPOINT: Understand what is needed.

Sometimes what is needed most in the kingdom of God is not what I'm most gifted for or what I'm most comfortable with. If this is the case, I must not limit the work of God to my preferences and comfort zone. Sometimes God directs our lives away from what is easiest and into areas that are more challenging. He does this to promote personal and spiritual growth. If I am only open to ministries that fit my preferences, then I might be missing an opportunity to grow as God desires.

From the earlier example: What if I like children, and I'm good with children, but there are 214 children's ministry workers in my church and no one to play the keyboard? Does my church need another children's ministry worker? Am I willing to meet the need of the Kingdom? Am I willing to pursue music and learn the keyboard to meet this need? Sometimes God will call us to fulfill the need in His kingdom, rather than just 'plugging us in' where we are already comfortable.

Chapter Five: **Where Is God Leading?**

When I was a teenager, I played the saxophone. I was fine playing in the orchestra pit or where no one could look at me directly. Yet when I was in plain view, I was terrified. I once tried to play a solo in front of our youth group and could never play a single note. I simply squeaked the entire time until I sat down embarrassed beyond measure. In those moments, my hands sweated so profusely that I could barely hold onto the saxophone. I was terrified to be in front of an audience. But that is who I used to be.

Today, I have been privileged to speak before audiences of more than fifteen thousand people. I've also addressed small congregations with ten or twelve in service. I have ministered in thirty-eight states, eight Canadian provinces, and nine countries. I have been privileged to speak at national meetings, conferences, camp meetings, ministers' training, youth camps and conventions, and various local church functions.

I can't imagine the things I would have missed had I only allowed God to use the things "I am" and not allowed Him to change the things "I'm not." I can't imagine what my life would be like if someone had not provoked me to live beyond my abilities, interests, and comfort zone. Thank God someone helped me to understand the need. Maybe God is directing you to minister in an area of need. Understand that in our selfish culture, it is a great testament to Christianity to sacrifice your personal interests in order to fill a Kingdom need.

> **WAYPOINT:** **Understand the power of your environment.**

Up to this point, the greatest portion of my ministry involvement has been to youth. I spent more than fifteen years in youth ministry. Roughly seven years ago I became involved in church planting in an administrative role. Not long after I started in this vein, I was in a small group discussion where we were considering methods to increase the number of church planters. We were talking about getting church planting onto the ministerial radar for more candidates. During this discussion, I began to think of my own experience. As I sat in that room and listened, I realized that I had never considered starting a church. Not once. At no point in my ministerial service had church planting been a consideration. Why not?

To answer that question, I began thinking about why I pursued youth ministry. And I realized that I became involved in youth ministry because I was in a youth ministry environment. As a young minister, in short order, the district youth leader pursued me and

Chapter Five: **Where Is God Leading?**

welcomed me into the collection of youth ministers. He invited me into the team. He encouraged me to be a part of his group. He brought me into that environment. (Thank you, Norman Paslay II!)

At the same time, at the church where I worked in Christian Education, there was a need for a new couple to join the youth team. My wife and I accepted an invitation. We didn't wake up at night with a compelling burden to pray for young people. We just did what was asked of us. And once involved, we began to pray over young people. Then we began to get involved in their lives. Then we started to read more on the subject of youth ministry. We became youth ministers. Why? The power of our environment.

Understand that environment can affect the fulfillment of your calling. As such, you can intentionally become involved in a specific environment, or you can say yes when invited to participate and allow the environment to shape your direction.

WAYPOINT: **Understand the value and purpose of education.**

First, a personal disclaimer: I am an absolute believer in education. I've never met people in their golden years who look

In Case You Were Wandering

back on their lives and say, "I wish I'd have quit school earlier." Those who reach their seventh and eighth decades realize that it is much easier to learn from others' successes and failures than to attempt to learn only through experience. This is just one of many reasons that I believe in formal education and training.

Of course, it is at this point that twentysomethings invariably pose questions regarding the type of education that they should pursue. This is a challenge somewhat unique to Christians as we have an additional consideration to pursue a college specifically aimed toward ministry—Bible college. Should I attend Bible college or a Christian college? Or should I attend a secular university? As explained previously, this is not a book designed to give answers, but rather a book that helps ask the right questions. The right answers to educational questions are found in the same fashion as the right answers to other life-direction questions. The previous chapters and paragraphs of this book can help in this educational choice as well. The previous few sections of this chapter are a good place to start: Understand who you are, what is needed, and the power of your environment. Thoughtful consideration of these

Chapter Five: **Where Is God Leading?**

few subjects provides a solid beginning toward making educational decisions.

WAYPOINT: **Understand God's priorities.**

Until now, much of this chapter has been spent on pragmatic understandings, but there are certainly some spiritual understandings that should be considered as well. In addressing the Romans, Paul wrote the following:

"I beseech you therefore, brethren, by the mercies of God, that you present your bodies a living sacrifice, holy, acceptable to God, which is your reasonable service. And do not be conformed to this world, but be transformed by the renewing of your mind, that you may prove what is that good and acceptable and perfect will of God" (Romans 12:1-2).

The phrase "that you may prove" what is the will of God lets us see that we are involved in this process of discovering God's direction for our lives. In the New Living Translation, the same verse includes the phrase "then you will learn to know God's will for you," which again suggests a process of understanding, growing, and discovering God's direction for our lives. It is further good to notice that the proving and learning of God's will comes after we have presented our bodies a living sacrifice and then allowed our minds to be renewed in order to transform our lives. In other words, there is a great deal of personal growth involved along with our pursuit of God's will.

Sometimes we get so focused on "the next step" or "what do I do now" that we lose our focus on simply becoming better Christians. We forget that God's priority is to transform our individual lives. His priority is to make us better people. Then as that takes place, we learn God's will for our lives. As my friend Nate Binion says, "Stop searching for the will of God and start allowing God to transform you." Understand that God is more interested in what we become than in where we are going.

WAYPOINT: **Understand the incredible value of spiritual disciplines.**

According to a George Barna study, twentysomethings are less likely than any other age group

- to attend church services,
- to donate to churches,

Chapter Five: **Where Is God Leading?**

- to be absolutely committed to Christianity,
- to read the Bible,
- or to serve as volunteers or lay leaders in churches.

Thus, the tendency in this life-stage is to look to other sources while negotiating our path. According to the same study, there are roughly eight million twentysomethings alive today who were active churchgoers as teenagers, but who will no longer be active in church by their thirtieth birthday. Please do not join the eight million.

Having realized God's priorities for our lives, we know that spiritual disciplines are valuable for what they teach me about God and His kingdom. Prayer and Bible study are valuable because they are used by God to mold and make me into His image. Worship and fasting are valuable to bring my human nature into alignment with His nature. Consistent involvement in a local congregation makes me accountable to Christian leaders and peers and also exposes me to biblical perspectives that I would not discover on my own. These things are not simply tools to get answers from God or to get God to do things for me. Rather, these practices are my fundamental resources for immersing my life in His purposes. Spiritual disciplines increase my knowledge of God and assist in my becoming who He wants me to be. The more I do this, the easier it is to know where He is leading me.

WAYPOINT: **Understand that a life spent fulfilling God's calling is simply a continual series of single steps in God's direction.**

"When you have a great and difficult task, something perhaps almost impossible, if you only work a little at a time, every day a little, suddenly the work will finish itself."
—Isak Dinesen

"A journey of a thousand miles begins with a single step."
—Lao-tzu

This statement is so simple and yet endures because it is so true. Rather than focus on life's path far off into the distance, we are better served to consistently make good choices for our next step. Get that accomplished and then simply face the step after that one. No need to fret over our step one thousand paces away, one hundred paces away, or ten paces away. Those steps that are so far removed present so many options and so many variables,

Chapter Five: **Where Is God Leading?**

that we can become paralyzed like the child in the candy store. Instead, let's rest our mind on the step right before us where the light is shining right at our feet. After all, the light is brightest up close, and that step is best illuminated by His knowledge. Or, as Nate Binion also says, "Commit to start wherever you are; the rest will happen." Doing something is better than doing nothing. So take a step in God's direction.

"Your word is a lamp to my feet and a light to my path" (Psalm 119:105).

Chapter Six:

Who's Going My Direction?

"Take care to get what you like, or you will be forced to like what you get."

—George Bernard Shaw

- **A Possible Scenario**

Jack and Jill have been sweethearts since junior high school and remain so through high school. As good Christians, they know to save sex for marriage. Yet their happy hormones are working overtime, and their convictions are too weak to keep them from fooling around. After enough of that, they end up pregnant. Though their convictions are not strong enough to practice self-control, they are strong enough to prevent them from killing the baby because of their mistake.

Since they have been sweethearts for so long, they see the pregnancy as sufficient reason to get married. So, they marry and a few months later their baby is born.

In Case You Were Wandering

Jill left school to have the baby, and having only a high school diploma, Jack works at a convenience store selling Slurpees. They are poor as dirt, so as soon as Jill can take the baby to her mom's for babysitting, she also gets a job.

Jack is content to sell Slurpees and play softball a couple of nights a week. Jill is not. She wants more out of life. After learning of a tuition-payment perk from her employer, she passes the General Education Development Test and starts community college part time. Jill loses a lot of sleep with the baby, working, and the course load, but she thoroughly enjoys classes. College is broadening her outlook on life and her possibilities for the future.

Jack loves that his softball team is doing well enough to make the playoffs and that his employer is providing new uniforms for the entire team.

After graduating with her bachelor's degree, Jill's employer awards her with a third promotion and offers to pay for her graduate studies. After another four years, she has earned her MBA and is leading an entire section at her accounting firm.

Jack has aged a bit. He cannot run the bases like he used to. But he can still pound one over the fence now and then.

Chapter Six: Who's Going My Direction?

This couple faces trouble.

Their marriage can survive, but it will be difficult and could involve one or both of them not being as fulfilled in life as they could have been had they married someone who was heading in the same direction as they were. Neither Jack nor Jill is good or bad, right or wrong; neither one is better than the other. However, they are clearly heading in different directions with their lives. If their walk with God does not remain strong, our culture is likely to prevail, and one of them will fall for a person who is heading in the same direction that they are: Jack for a team fan or Jill for an account manager.

This is not a chapter on dating. Instead, it offers some relationship material as guideposts for healthy relationships that lead to marriage. Of course, to present this assumes you are now at the stage of life where you are not simply dating to become comfortable in social settings with the opposite sex, but you are entering into relationships in an attempt to find a spouse.

To this assumption you might reply, "Hey! I am not looking to get married!" Most likely, you are. Maybe not today, or in the next couple of weeks, but for most, this life-stage involves discovering the type of person with whom you will spend the rest of your life. Being more mature, you have a greater ability to look toward the future, a clearer understanding of who you are, and a more complete picture of God's direction for your life. So, take care to find someone who is going your direction.

WAYPOINT: **The more homogeneous the relationship is, the greater the chance of marital satisfaction.**

A homogeneous relationship is one that enjoys a number of "sames." Such a relationship could have the same family structures, the same religious convictions, the same career goals, the same recreational likes, and the same cultural backgrounds. The more "sames" there are in the relationship, the more likely the marriage is to succeed and be fulfilling.

Unfortunately, there are no guarantees, but we increase the chances in our favor by increasing the "sames." Sameness occurs in people who are going in the same direction in their lives. Along this path of discovery, there are some relational waypoints that can help us find that person.

Chapter Six: Who's Going My Direction?

WAYPOINT: **Discover your differences and commonalities.**

While reading the previous paragraphs, a common saying may have come to mind: "Opposites attract." It is a catchy phrase that has been quoted for years, regularly used to explain or excuse some relationships. There is also a corollary to that phrase that is not so oft quoted: "Opposites also tend to attack." Though initially attracted to each other, opposites are not as likely to make good spouses. Again, a greater number of commonalities increases the likelihood of success. Talkative extroverts will struggle spending the rest of their lives with silent introverts. One enjoys people, places, and social activity while the other is completely happy being absolutely alone for great periods of time. One of the keys to fulfilling marriages is spending time together. If your recreational desires are diametrically opposed, it is going to be difficult to spend time in each other's company. It is best to be intellectually honest with yourself and recognize significant differences like these in advance.

And what are the things that you have in common? Are there significant commonalities? Take a close look at the family heritage for each of you. Find out about each other's family history and the various successes and failures in each. Are there favorable similarities? Maybe he is one of seven siblings and you are an only child. Have either of you considered how large you would like your family to be? Do you have a common vision for children? When you visit each other's families, pay close attention to how parents interact. How does his dad treat his mom? How does his mom treat his dad? Are her mom and dad still married? What are his role expectations? How does she think a husband should treat a wife? How does he think a wife should treat a husband? What are some defining things about your parents' relationships? Do you want a relationship like that, or something different? So many questions seem like a homework assignment. Exactly. The assignment is to discover commonalities.

And what about church? You may have met your special someone at a regional event, over the Internet, or through a mutual friend. If you live far enough away from each other that your time together is limited, it is particularly important that you spend time visiting each other's churches and discovering how this person responds in her own congregation. She might talk of being very faithful to her local congregation. To you "very faithful" means being in service every time the doors are open. To her, it might mean that she attends every holiday and for some other special occasions. If this is the case, do you really have a common appreciation for a local congregation? This is something that you need to discover.

Chapter Six: Who's Going My Direction?

No couple enters marriage with zero differences. There are some differences that are known prior to marriage, and there are some that are revealed as the relationship progresses over the years. Certainly couples can and do remain close when there are differences, but it requires one or both to make course corrections. Commitment to the marriage empowers that willingness to change. But prior to marriage, while searching for that one who is going your direction, it is best to examine the differences and their significance prior to the vows.

WAYPOINT: **What commonalities and differences really matter?**

We must acknowledge that we will have both commonalities and differences; then we must think through these questions:
- Are the differences big enough to send us in different directions?
- Are the commonalities strong enough to keep us going in the same direction?

To illustrate this point, consider a difference that can be challenging in some circles: interracial marriages. As has been shown in many relationships across North America, interracial

In Case You Were Wandering

marriages can be successful. And personally, I cannot fault them as a whole. But in your life, what I think is not what is most important.

I am in favor of sameness in relationships. If the couple is interracial, there had better be many more "sames" in their relationship. Culture is powerful. A person from one race who was raised in metropolitan Toronto can have serious difficulty in a relationship with a person of the same race who was raised in rural Louisiana, because their cultures are so different. If a Hispanic man who has recently immigrated to the United States from rural Mexico enters a relationship with a Hispanic woman whose family has lived in southern California for three generations, there could be cultural trouble. Though of the same race, southern Californian culture has a much different regard for women than rural Mexican culture. Their pending distress has nothing to do with skin color, but everything to do with culture.

Are the differences big enough to send you in different directions?

Are the commonalities strong enough to keep you going in the same direction?

Christian proponents of interracial marriage often point to Moses, a Jew, who married an Ethiopian woman (Numbers 12).

Chapter Six: Who's Going My Direction?

Those who reference this example must also note that Aaron and Miriam, Moses' brother and sister, were angry with him over the marriage. In the same fashion, you might be totally at ease entering into an interracial marriage. But what does your family think? What do your friends think? What does your pastor think? What about the community you will live in? Will they accept you, or reject you? What is allowable may not always be preferable. As with a marriage between those of different races, there are some additional and sometimes bigger questions that have to be explored. Take the time needed to evaluate the size of your differences and the strength of your commonalities.

> **WAYPOINT:** **Appearance and affection are cheap substitutes for personality and character.**

I remember a time when our older daughter was beginning to attract the attention of young men. Of course, she has always attracted their attention, but I recall the time when she became interested in returning their attention. For some reason, I felt compelled to share with her a statement that I had been sharing with teens for some time. So, one evening during a comfortable discussion about relationships, I told her this: "'He's cute' and 'He likes me' are never sufficient reasons to like a boy." Looks and affection are not enough.

Popular culture is lying to this generation. Happy relationships are not based solely on appearance. If so, the prominent pretty people plastered across billboards, magazines, and screens everywhere should have the very best relationships mankind can offer. Instead Hollywood, which glowingly promotes the "pretty people are valuable" concept, is littered with beautiful couples whose marriages end in bitter divorce. Happy relationships are not based solely on appearance.

That is not to say that we should shun appealing appearance. If you can find appearance *and* character (like I did), more power to you. But in terms of value to your relationship, character and personality are of much greater value than appearance and affection.

As for affection, receiving it from another is a powerful human desire. We enjoy the affection of others. It is human and natural. And it is not wrong. However, another's affection for me does not dictate my life direction. This applies to all friendships, not just companionships. The primary reason for my relationship with someone must never be based solely on that person's affection for me. Rather, I enter into and maintain friendships and relationships

Chapter Six: Who's Going My Direction?

based on that person's life proceeding in the same direction as my own. On this premise, I choose my friends; I do not let my friends choose me. The same holds true for relationships.

This is an important conviction because of the power of affection. Our life-direction has to take priority over our need for affection. If my God-calling can be derailed by the affection of the un-called, then I should not be surprised when the enemy sends such a person my way. My need for affection must not derail my God-called direction. We should not be so desperate for someone that we lose who we are. My God-called direction is most important.

After explaining this waypoint to my daughter in our discussion, she had an impacting experience that I believe was a blessing from God. Within a week of our talk, she was eating lunch with a bunch of her friends. As often happens with girls of that age, the discussion turned to relationships with young men. Not long into the topic, one of my daughter's friends clearly declared, "All that matters to me is, 'Is he cute?' and 'Does he like me?'" When sharing this story with her mother and me, it was abundantly clear that our daughter realized that some people have very low relationship expectations. Further, she declared that her expectations would be higher.

I hope you will do the same.

In Case You Were Wandering

WAYPOINT: **Take your time. Slow down. What's the hurry?**

You might respond, "We are going slowly." Good. Can you go slower? The average age of marriage in the United States today is about twenty-six for women and twenty-eight for men. Why does it seem like some Christians are trying so hard to lower those averages? When finding, choosing, and marrying the person with whom I will spend the rest of my life, it stands to reason that this is not a decision that is to be made quickly. In fact, in many traditional wedding ceremonies, we still hear the officiating minister intone that "marriage is not to be entered into unadvisedly or lightly, but reverently, deliberately, and in accordance with the purposes for which it was instituted by God." This is a serious decision, a serious commitment. We should take the time to get this right.

Some might argue that those outside of Christianity marry later in life because they are having sex before marriage. Therefore, they can wait longer to be married. I will agree that may have something to do with the higher average ages of marriage in the United States; however, sex should not be our primary reason for marriage. Certainly it is a powerful perk, but it must not be the primary reason for marriage. One insightful twentysomething

Chapter Six: Who's Going My Direction?

shared this observation with my daughter: "Getting married for the sex is like flying in a plane for the peanuts." When a couple marries for the sex, they are marrying for the act and not for the person. Just like flying in a plane is about so much more than the snacks, so is a person, and a marriage, about much more than the sex.

Take your time. Discover the right person to marry.

Further, we should take time to discover the right emotions for marriage. Did you know that infatuation fades after roughly two years? It is true. A number of relationship writers and social scientists have recognized a differentiation between emotions of "falling in love" and the "real love" that maintains a marriage. Though different authors use different terms, the basic understanding is that the infatuation that occurs when falling in love is based only in emotions, tends to disengage reasoning, and lasts about two years. In contrast, real love is emotional in nature, but not totally emotional. Real love unites reason with the emotion. It involves an act of the will and requires discipline and effort. Real love is an action, much more than a feeling. Based on my commitment to another, I treat them in a fashion that communicates my love for them. The resulting emotion is real love.

In Case You Were Wandering

Based on this knowledge, marrying during that first two years of infatuation does not allow a couple to discover whether or not they have progressed into genuine love that is based on commitment and choice. This is another reason to extend the time spent getting to know each other prior to marriage. If a couple can extend the time that they spend in courtship and engagement to a period of roughly two years, then they are more likely to have entered into real love as they begin marriage. Incidentally, roughly 50 percent of divorces take place after about two years of marriage—after infatuation wears off.

Slow down. Discover the right person and the right reasons to marry.

WAYPOINT: **Keep your brain in the game.**

My hobby is cycling. I recently finished reading an article in a cycling magazine that discussed the mental aspect of the sport. One article included interviews with some regarded trainers and sports physicians who cannot explain all of the physical aspects of winners. They continue to recognize that there are some athletes who are simply more mentally disciplined than others. In fact,

Chapter Six: Who's Going My Direction?

there are some cyclists whose physical attributes are below those of other leading riders; however, they continue to compete at the highest level. The only explanation provided is mental discipline. These riders are not overwhelmed by any of the various elements that hinder others: weather, fatigue, equipment failure, team dissonance, and so on. Instead, they use their minds to overcome their actions, rather than succumb to mere feelings and circumstances. These winners are able to keep their minds in the race.

Those who are able to navigate successfully the various dimensions of relationships are those who keep their brains in the game. Twentysomethings are at their best in a relationship when they use their reasoning to balance their emotions. No, we cannot address relationships as purely mental or mechanical, but neither can we engage them from a purely emotional state. At our best, we involve both aspects to develop a healthy relationship. When discovering that right person, there are many items to observe.

Observe her honesty. At the very core of every successful relationship is trust. Relationships can survive many challenges, but a lack of trust is very difficult to overcome. As such, honesty is a primary virtue in a potential spouse. Pay attention to how she practices honesty. Observe her actions in comparison to her words. Note the reasons that she gives for mistakes or shortcomings. If you sense that there is a dissonance between her words and actions, bring it up in discussion. Some do this intentionally, and some just cannot recognize the disconnect between their words and their actions. Whatever the reason, this is trouble. When a person lacks integrity, which is a character flaw, it is a significant problem. How a person handles the truth is a very important skill that must be considered.

Discuss and observe his life-direction and vision. If you intend to be an overseas missionary and he plans to live within a three-mile radius of his childhood home, that discrepancy needs to be discussed and resolved. Additionally, observe whether he is living consistent with his stated direction. Is he walking the walk or just talking the talk? He may speak enthusiastically about being an astronaut, but he is twenty-seven years old and has yet to enroll in university or join the air force. Are his ambitions genuine, or is he simply mimicking your ambitions to create a false commonality? You will obtain answers to these questions when you observe his actions to be sure that they match his words.

Chapter Six: Who's Going My Direction?

Observe his desire and ability to communicate. Building the trust necessary to venture into discussions that involve closely held areas is likely to take some time. If the relationship continues beyond a year and he is still not revealing much of his true thoughts and feelings, then know this: it will not get better after you get married. Walking down the marriage aisle does not miraculously change a person's personality, communication skills, or character traits. It is important to know challenges of the person you will marry.

Observe friendships. Spend time with each other's friends. Talk about the things each of you value about your friends. If either of you does not enjoy the company of the other's friends, then discuss the reasons and possible solutions. His friends were there before you, and they are likely to remain. Observe each other's actions within group settings. Watch how she interacts with her friends, how she interacts with your friends, and how you all interact together. Are her actions consistent in each setting? If not, can she explain why? How does she treat the people that you care about? What do your friends think about the two of you being together? If upon your engagement her friends say, "She's been engaged four times now. We're used to this," how will you respond? Do you think "Yikes!" or "I'm different than those four other guys"? Observe friendships and keep your mind in the game.

In Case You Were Wandering

Suppose that when leaving church this Sunday, you decide to walk home as it is only a few blocks away. It is not too far, and you want to enjoy the walk. With the belief that you can follow your innate sense of direction and the many warm feelings that you have for your family and home, you decide to walk to the house blindfolded. At this point, lots of things can happen. You might walk directly and safely to your home. Or you might trip and fall—maybe a number of times. You might bump into a lot of cars. You might walk off an embankment at the edge of the lot and fall onto the concrete sidewalk below. Or, you might just walk out onto the street into oncoming traffic and be hit by a car. Though you have a natural sense of direction and many warm feelings for your family, the best way to walk to your house is to simply take off the blindfold. Keeping your brain in the game is like taking off that blindfold. It adds a much-needed advantage to our innate senses and our warm feelings.

WAYPOINT: **Marriage is the long-term relationship you need to keep.**

The corollary to this statement is: relationships not leading to marriage need not be long term. Since you know your life's direction, when you meet someone and spend some time with

Chapter Six: **Who's Going My Direction?**

them, you can fairly quickly get a sense of who they are and where they are going. If these are not compatible with your life-direction, then why would you continue the relationship? Why spend months or years with someone whom you are not thinking of marrying?

The more time spent in a relationship, the more difficult it is to end and to get over. Knowing this, you should quickly end relationships with someone who is not going your direction. The longer you remain attached and build emotional ties, the harder it is to end an unpromising relationship. The lesson then is to discern the person's direction as quickly as possible and based on that knowledge, keep or toss.

Ignoring this fact, some continue relationships for the companionship. They have grown accustomed to having someone with them to attend various functions, to talk with regularly, and to share recreational activities. It is not recommended to continue a relationship solely for the companionship. While companionship is valuable, you can have numerous friendships and camaraderie without being in a dating relationship. If the person is not pursuing the same life direction, do not maintain that relationship just for the companionship.

Some continue in mismatched relationships because they have wrongly bought into our culture's mores. They keep the relationship for the physical intimacy. The sex. Obviously, saving all intimacy for marriage is the best thing for any relationship.

According to Scripture, as a single person, this is the rule regarding sex:
Sex only within marriage.

According to Scripture, as a married person, this is the rule regarding sex:
Sex only within marriage.

Of course, it is the same rule for both circumstances: both situations require self-control. Whether within or outside the confines of marriage, Christians are called to control their sexual impulses. It is either sex with no person or sex with one person. Both situations demand self-control. The smart thing to do is to practice self-control over your sexual impulses now so that you will be able to confidently pledge the same to your spouse when you are married.

When couples are involved sexually prior to marriage, it creates relational confusion. Sex was created to solidify the marriage commitment. Beyond the physical act, there are strong emotional bonds created by sex. When a person creates those bonds with someone other than a spouse, someone who is not traveling on

Chapter Six: Who's Going My Direction?

the same lifelong path, it forms emotional ties that make it very difficult to evaluate the relationship intellectually. It makes it more difficult to keep your brain in the game. Yes, according to the Bible, sex outside of marriage is sin. But also, saving sex for marriage reduces relational confusion and mistakes. It is the smart thing to do.

Consider Samson. How could he have been so stupid? Have you ever thought about that? When Delilah asked him about the source of his strength the first time, he told her a lie. When he woke up, he had been tied up with brand new ropes—just what he told her. She asked again, he lied again, and when he woke up, his hair was braided—just what he told her. Couldn't he have seen a pattern there? She kept asking until he told her the truth. When he woke up, they had shaved his head; he lost his strength and was captured by the Philistines. How could Samson have been so clueless?

Well, he kept visiting Delilah in her tent. Alone. When she was asking him all the questions, his head was in her lap. Each time he woke up, he was in her tent. What does it sound like to you? It sounds to me like he was sleeping with her. Samson was so stupid because his reasoning was clouded by his emotions, his hormones, and the sex. Saving sex for marriage is smarter than that.

In Case You Were Wandering

But if you have already made this mistake, and you are remaining in a relationship simply because of sex, you have a decision to make. Is the mistake of getting physically involved before marriage a good enough reason to keep dating the wrong person, or to marry the wrong person? This caution is basically to the ladies, because way too many guys have no problem basing a relationship only on sex. As a lady you might be tempted to allow the intimacy so that you can keep him, or believing that in time he will change and his life will start going in your direction. Maybe. Maybe you will also win $200 million in the lottery. If your life and his life are clearly heading in different directions, it will be easier to bail out now rather than later. Marriage is the long-term relationship you need to keep.

WAYPOINT: **Breaking up is hard to do.**

At this point, since I have recommended ending fruitless relationships, it would be good to offer a few words about breaking up. As the songwriter penned, "Breaking up is hard to do." Yes, this can be true. But it must be done if the person you are with is not the right person. I am not going to attempt to give you the words to say, but I am going to point out some things not to say. When

Chapter Six: **Who's Going My Direction?**

ending a relationship, please do not use the Christian standby: "It is not God's will that we be together." I would love to know how many readers laughed when they read that phrase. Please, quit taking the lazy way out and using God as a shortcut for expressing your true feelings and explaining the deficiencies you see in the relationship.

There are two easily observed problems with this slothful strategy. First, what happens if the two of you work out your differences and end up back together? Did God change His mind? If not, are you now pursuing a relationship that you know is not God's plan for your life? As you can see, employing the "not God's will" strategy is a problem. Maybe God did speak to you. Maybe He has made it clear to you that you must end this relationship; however, do not use this as the easy way to unload someone. Be more mature and more honest than that. Second, when we take the time to express our true feelings and give the person clear reasons why we are ending the relationship, then we each have opportunities to grow. If he feels like he has to end the relationship due to her inability to successfully address conflict, he needs to tell her that so that she can prayerfully consider this observation and grow to become a better person. If she feels that his Christian devotion is not strong enough for her, he needs to know this so that he can address this opinion and have opportunity to grow. When we use the "not God's will" strategy, we short-circuit an opportunity for another Christian to grow as an individual. So while breaking up might be hard to do, please take the time to give detailed reasons for your decision.

WAYPOINT: **Take advantage of premarital counseling.**

Hopefully, the church you attend provides or even requires that engaged couples participate in premarital counseling. These sessions are an opportunity to obtain relational training, glean insights on your relationship from an objective observer, and gather wisdom from spiritual leadership that has vested interest in your marital success. Ideally, these sessions will be presented by the pastor or a member of the pastoral team. Though there are myriad details involved in preparing for the wedding and your future life together, it is very important that each one of you participate wholeheartedly in this endeavor. Premarital counseling is a wonderful opportunity to discover the strengths and weaknesses of your relationship.

Though many congregations have preferred timing for the sessions, a couple should consider beginning the sessions very soon after the engagement, rather than in the weeks just prior to the wedding. In this way, in the event that some seriously

Chapter Six: Who's Going My Direction?

challenging areas are discovered, the couple is freer to postpone the wedding date, or cancel the engagement entirely if necessary. Making such decisions closer to the wedding date can be much more difficult once the invitations have been mailed, the hall has been rented, and the caterer has been paid. Earlier premarital sessions make a difficult decision a little easier. Marriage is a lifelong commitment in the sight of God. It is one of the biggest decisions that any individual will make. If you are not sure at least postpone it, and do not be afraid to call it off. It is much better to be embarrassed, disappointed, and even talked about than to marry the wrong person. Premarital counseling is sure to benefit your relationship, and in a few cases, it can also prevent some from making a mistake.

WAYPOINT: **Who's going your direction?**

Nancy Astor was the first woman to sit as a member of parliament in the British House of Commons. She is also known for her sarcastic wit and its use in exchanges with Prime Minister Winston Churchill. In one exchange attributed to these politicians during a social function, Nancy Astor intoned to Prime Minister

In Case You Were Wandering

Churchill, "If I were your wife, I would poison your coffee!" To which he retorted, "And if I were your husband, I would surely drink it."

While clearly witty, the sentiments of each represent something twentysomethings should avoid when choosing a lifetime spouse. To do so, we can rely on a variety of waypoints to discover someone who is going our direction.

Chapter Seven:

Ignoring Accountability

"The safest road to Hell is the gradual one—the gentle slope, soft underfoot, without sudden turnings, without milestones, without signposts."

—*C. S. Lewis*

"The way of a fool is right in his own eyes, But he who heeds counsel is wise" (Proverbs 12:15).

"Every way of a man is right in his own eyes, But the Lord weighs the hearts" (Proverbs 21:2).

"One person esteems one day above another; another esteems every day alike. Let each be fully convinced in his own mind. He who observes the day, observes it to the Lord; and he who does not observe the day, to the Lord he does not observe it. He who eats, eats to the Lord, for he gives God thanks; and he who does not eat, to the Lord he does not eat, and gives God thanks. For none of us lives to himself, and no one dies to himself. For if we live, we live to the Lord; and if we die, we die to the Lord.

In Case You Were Wandering

Therefore, whether we live or die, we are the Lord's. For to this end Christ died and rose and lived again, that He might be Lord of both the dead and the living. But why do you judge your brother? Or why do you show contempt for your brother? For we shall all stand before the judgment seat of Christ. For it is written: 'As I live, says the Lord,

Every knee shall bow to Me, And every tongue shall confess to God.' So then each of us shall give account of himself to God. Therefore let us not judge one another anymore, but rather resolve this, not to put a stumbling block or a cause to fall in our brother's way (Romans 14:5-13).

The verses from Proverbs provide an unfavorable slant on being "right in our own eyes." We learn that there is something about humans that causes us to tend to trust in our own understanding, our own thoughts, and our own way. We like to believe we are right. We like to believe we have all the answers. We like to think we can solve all problems and make all decisions on our own. We seek and embrace independence. But the Bible calls this foolish.

Then the writer of Romans asserted that no one lives to himself or dies to himself and that we will all give account of our lives to God. Clearly, we cannot be totally independent when none of us lives to himself or dies to himself. Neither are we completely independent to pursue our own ways when we are destined to give

Chapter Seven: Ignoring Accountability

account of our lives to God. In both the Old Testament and the New Testament, the Word of God addresses this tendency of mankind to pursue independence and shun accountability. Something within the human makeup causes us to be susceptible to ignoring the counsel of others and of God. In the end, independence is a facade. No one lives alone or dies alone. We will all give account of our lives to God. Every individual will stand before the righteous Judge of all mankind and be called to give explanation and justification for the manner in which he lived his life. Accountability is inevitable.

From the moment we are born, we begin maturing toward adulthood. The process is quite slow. It takes many years. It takes the collective investment of many loving and wise adults God places into our lives. As the maturity process proceeds we seek and obtain greater independence. We learn to ask for food

In Case You Were Wandering

that we like, rather than just waiting until mom feeds us the creamed peas. We learn to walk about on our own, rather than being carried by dad, or wheeled in a stroller. Wise parents begin early to establish in our understanding the connection between responsibility and independence. Thus, as maturity compels us to greater independence, we are required to display responsibility in our use of it. As we prove responsible, we are granted further independence. Mom allows me to play outside independently most of the day when I am responsible to remain within the backyard. Dad allows me to mow the lawn on the riding mower when I can be trusted not to mow over mom's flowers. Maturity continues to feed the desire for independence while responsibility continues to provide for it. Over the years, as we further approach adulthood, we become more and more independent of the authoritative adults around us. We are trusted to spend weeks away at summer camp. We are trusted to complete homework assignments. As we continue to successfully handle independence our confidence grows to handle it in different and varied situations. Soon we confidently learn to drive. We independently hold a part-time job. And before we know it, we graduate from high school to pursue our culture's respected commencement into a new and greater dimension of independence.

And this is when too many young adults veer onto the detour of ignored accountability.

Chapter Seven: Ignoring Accountability

Somehow, as we make this transition into adulthood, we struggle to successfully maintain accountability in our lives. Moving out of our parents' household, stepping into total self-sufficiency for our food, shelter, and clothing, we are frequently unable to properly sustain accountability for how we live. Though we are no longer under direct parental authority, the Scripture clearly notes that we will be held accountable for our lives. As such, there must be a method for twentysomethings to live within spiritual accountability while fully embracing independent adulthood. We have to prevent living as though we are "right in our own eyes" and be prepared to answer to God all while espousing self-determining adulthood. How can we do that?

WAYPOINT: **New accountability is needed.**

When we leave the accountability of parental authority, it is exceedingly important to replace that accountability with new forms of accountability: situational accountability and human accountability. At its core, accountability is the practice of making yourself answerable to others. It is the practice of keeping yourself vulnerable to the awareness of others. Christians do this intentionally in order to direct our lives to good things and to better things. We also do this to protect ourselves from sin.

In Case You Were Wandering

Situational accountability is just what it sounds like: situations that make us the most accountable. Within situational accountability, there are different aspects. We consider our location and the time of day when speaking of situational accountability. Specifically, location refers to whether or not our setting is public or private. We make ourselves more accountable when we are in public places. There is a greater likelihood of someone walking by, of someone seeing us, and of someone being aware of our actions. Just the opposite is true in private settings. This is the reasoning behind recommending that families keep their desktop computers in the family room, the kitchen, or some other frequently visited area of the house. In this way, while we are using the computer, we make ourselves vulnerable to anyone who might be passing by the screen as I use the machine. I make myself accountable via public location. In a similar fashion, there is greater situational accountability in relation to the time of day. Think about some of these questions:

- What time of day are most crimes committed and arrests made?

Chapter Seven: Ignoring Accountability

- What time of day is most associated with drinking? With illicit sexual activity?
- What time of day is associated with the most frightening scenes in stories?

Night. There is something about the darkness that diminishes man's inhibitions. The later it is at night, the more likely humans are to be involved in actions, words, and practices that they would normally not pursue in the daylight. Under the cover of night, we reason that it is more difficult for others to see us participating in bad behaviors. We are emboldened toward wrongdoing, toward evil, by the cover of nightfall. Knowing this, we practice situational accountability by limiting the times that we are active at night and increasing the times we are active during the day. Our best situational accountability is in a public place during the brightest time of the day.

Although as independent adults we are no longer under the direct authority of our parents, we still need to rely on humans to bring accountability into our lives. The effectiveness of human accountability rests on two factors: the quantity of humans around me and the quality of humans around me. Quantity is quite easy to understand. The more people that are involved in any situation, the more likely someone will witness any wrong action on my part. The fewer people around, the likelihood of my actions being discovered diminishes. You know this. It is the reason that men and women who are committing adultery seek out locations where they are not likely to be recognized. Twentysomethings at a party who are interested in sexual behavior do not search out the more populated rooms at the venue. No, they search for a place where they can be alone. More people present yields greater accountability for my actions.

In turn, it is not just the number of people in a circumstance that increases accountability; it is the quality of people involved. Attending a party consisting of faithful church members provides much more accountability than attending a party at a university frat house. The caliber of people we are with makes a difference in the accountability we receive. Quality humans make a difference in our actions. While we may not live at home any longer, there are still important people who should minister accountability into our lives. It may go without saying, but it still needs to be repeated: We bring ourselves into far better care when we willingly make ourselves accountable to spiritual leadership in our lives. Pastors, small group leaders, seasoned saints, and others provide us with the best type of human accountability available. When it comes to human accountability we are much more vulnerable, and therefore safe, when we pursue situations that include more people who are of greater quality.

Chapter Seven: Ignoring Accountability

WAYPOINT: **Better safe than vulnerable.**

Thus, the safest circumstance for being most personally accountable is in a public place, with a large number of mentors present, in the middle of the day. Conversely, the most vulnerable situation is a private place, in the presence of a small number of peers, late at night. When we desire to bypass the detour of ignored accountability and prevent being "right in our own eyes," here are four questions to guide our choices.

- Where will I be? (The more public the place, the better.)
- Who will be there? (The more quality people, the better.)
- How many people will be there? (The larger the crowd, the better.)
- What time will we be together? (The earlier in the day, the better.)

Regularly taking advantage of questions like these is what prepares us for the day when we will give account of our lives to God. Do not veer from your God-ordained direction onto the detour of ignored accountability. Instead, learn how to practice personal accountability now and continue to discover the path God has you traveling.

Chapter Eight:

Wasting Time

How many times have we been guilty of saying, "I don't have the time" when asked to do something for the kingdom of God? Usually we are sincere, but I wonder if it is always factual? Is it true that I simply have too many things scheduled? Or, is it truer that I have placed other things in a greater priority and therefore do not have the time to do more for God? Could it be that the statement "I don't have the time" has become an easy excuse not to commit to the service of the Lord? Who is going to challenge me on the statement? Who is going to follow me around all day to validate my schedule? Only I really know how busy I am. Paul challenged the Ephesians to make the most of every opportunity (Ephesians 5:16). To find out whether I am making the most of my opportunities, or wasting my time, will take some self-examination. It is a worthy exam as there are many twentysomethings whose journey is hindered by this pothole.

When considering the subject of time, it is good to remember God established and respects time (Genesis 1:14; Ecclesiastes 3:1). In fact, the Scripture has plenty to say about time. There are

In Case You Were Wandering

over seven hundred references to time in the King James Version and nearly one thousand references in the New International Version. Just under one hundred times "hour" is referenced: fifteen in Daniel and Revelation, eleven in Acts, and sixty-seven in the Gospels. Seeing that two-thirds of the New Testament references to "hour" are in the Gospels, evidently, Jesus was concerned about the time. We should be also.

In addition to Paul's Ephesian challenge, the writer of Ecclesiastes wrote that a wise man discerns both time and judgment (8:5). A wise man knows the appropriate time and places great value upon his time. He does this because he recognizes that the exact amount of time he has on this Earth is unknown.

Job posed these questions: "Is there not an appointed time to man upon earth? Are not his days also like the days of an hireling?" (Job 7:1, KJV). The fuller meaning of this passage rests in understanding the work of a hireling. A hireling is employed until the job is complete, not necessarily for a specific amount of time, much like we would hire a contractor today. We hire him to put on a roof, mow the lawn, or install carpeting, regardless of how long the job takes. Likewise, according to Job, our very lives are given as an amount of time to get the job done, not as a definite number of years. Knowing this begs the question: what is the job that I am to complete?

Chapter Eight: Wasting Time

Rick Warren posits, "You have just enough time to do God's will." God's will is both general and specific. Not everyone is directed to be a Sunday school teacher, but all are called to salvation. While each individual's God-ordained path is different, the general tasks are the same. The primary task of every man is to establish his eternal destination. Thus, all men are given enough time to choose between Heaven and Hell. Time must be used wisely.

WAYPOINT: **Time is in my possession.**

When considering personal time management, consider viewing time in a possessive sense. In Matthew 26:18, Jesus said, "My time is at hand; I will keep the Passover at thy house with my disciples" (KJV). He spoke of time as being in His possession; He said "my time." He was aware of a specific point in time that was of particular importance to Him. He had a certain assignment, a specific time to begin the project, and an allotted amount of time to get the job finished. It was His time. When we think of time in this fashion, it signifies accepting our responsibility for personal management of that time.

Having accepted the value of time and my responsibility to manage it, I have to ask, "How am I using my time?" With the given amount of time that I have, what tasks get the most of it? It has been said that you can tell a person's beliefs by how he spends his money and she spends her time. If that is the case, in what do I believe?

WAYPOINT: Spend the most time on the things that matter most.

Jesus rebuked men because they could predict tomorrow's weather, but they could not notice the value of His being with them on the Earth (Luke 12:56). Paul criticized the Athenians because they spent their time talking only about news events (Acts 17:21). In both cases, the point is being made that men were not using their time wisely. How much time do we spend talking about "some new thing"? There always seems to be some new tidbit of gossip, some new fashion statement, or a hot tech item. If we are not careful, we too could spend all of our time simply discussing new things. Paul commanded the Romans to wake up (Romans 13:11). In terms of spiritual endeavors, they were not at all in tune with the times. Evidently the human capacity to get priorities out of order is not a new one. Time is a personal commodity; therefore, the things that matter throughout eternity had better get the most of our time.

WAYPOINT: **Take control of your time.**

In order to accomplish this, there are some basic principles that work very effectively to keep us on track. The first is to prioritize according to eternity. "But seek ye first the kingdom of God, and his righteousness; and all these things shall be added unto you" (Matthew 6:33, KJV). Our daily activities need to be placed in order of importance based on God's Word and prayer. We look at our schedules and determine what is going to matter for eternity. When the day is done, how much have we accomplished to further the kingdom of God?

The second principle is to schedule our time according to godly priorities. Though basic, it is often overlooked. Scheduling is a biblical concept. We find the Lord often speaking of various appointments that He set and kept (Exodus 9:5; Daniel 11:29; Habakkuk 2:3; Galatians 4:2; Psalm 102:13). If God makes and keeps appointments, then undoubtedly we can do the same. Set a schedule and stick to it.

Another basic principle is to budget my time according to reality. How much time should we allow for each activity in our schedules? Important tasks lose out when we do not correctly gauge how long a particular activity will take. Will it take us thirty minutes or one hour to do laundry? Does it take twenty or thirty minutes to drive to church? Throughout Scripture, we notice specific time frames attached to appointments and schedules (Exodus 23:15; I Samuel 13:8; II Samuel 24:15; Esther 9:27). Perhaps Nehemiah set the best example: "And the king said unto me, (the queen also sitting by him,) For how long shall thy journey be? and when wilt thou return? So it pleased the king to send me; and I set him a time" (Nehemiah 2:6, KJV). In everyday practice, it's best to allow more time per event than necessary and end the day with time to spare, rather than to allow too little time and end up not accomplishing what we set out to do. It is best to budget time according to reality.

Conversely, as some may already be thinking, there are some things that cannot and will not be scheduled. Birth (Genesis 18:14), sin (Deuteronomy 32:35), blessing (I Peter 5:6), death (Genesis 38:12), and trouble (Psalm 27:5) are just some of the things noted in Scripture that typically are not scheduled exactly.

The same is true for some things in our lives. When we realize and accept the fact that there will be things that we cannot control, then we save ourselves from unnecessary frustration. We should do all that we can to redeem our time and then accept the things that we simply cannot control.

> **WAYPOINT:** **God works outside of the boundaries of time.**

For many of us, regardless of how well we adhere to these principles, we experience seasons when we have a genuine shortage of time. When this happens, remember God is not limited to time. In II Kings 20, God signaled His answer to Hezekiah by turning time back ten degrees. In Joshua 10, God stopped the sun and the moon so that the armies of Israel would have sufficient time to win their battle. Concerning God's perspective on time, Peter wrote, "But, beloved, be not ignorant of this one thing, that one day is with the Lord as a thousand years, and a thousand years as one day" (II Peter 3:8, KJV). God is not limited to time! Further we are promised, "If ye abide in me, and my words abide in you, ye shall ask what ye will, and it shall be done unto you" (John 15:7, KJV). Thus, when we are in a bind and have done our best, we can go to the Lord and ask Him to help us to be more efficient and to accomplish all that we need to do for His kingdom.

Time is in our hands. There is so much yet to be accomplished for God in our world. When we keep these two facts in the forefront of our minds, we are compelled to use practical tools to make sure we are using our time wisely.

Otherwise we might be detoured by wasting time.

Chapter Nine:

Foiled by Frustration

"Do not fret because of evildoers, Nor be envious of the workers of iniquity. For they shall soon be cut down like the grass, And wither as the green herb. Trust in the Lord, and do good; Dwell in the land, and feed on His faithfulness. Delight yourself also in the Lord, And He shall give you the desires of your heart. Commit your way to the Lord, Trust also in Him, And He shall bring it to pass. He shall bring forth your righteousness as the light, And your justice as the noonday. Rest in the Lord, and wait patiently for Him; Do not fret because of him who prospers in his way, Because of the man who brings wicked schemes to pass. Cease from anger, and forsake wrath; Do not fret—it only causes harm. For evildoers shall be cut off; But those who wait on the Lord, They shall inherit the earth. For yet a little while and the wicked shall be no more; Indeed, you will look carefully for his place, But it shall be no more" (Psalm 37:1-10).

For some people, life goes by without any challenges whatsoever. They are never disappointed, never frustrated, never experience setbacks. All of their expectations are realized and all of their dreams come true. Each day they experience clear and measurable progress toward the great things they envision for their lives.

Then there are the rest of us.

While we do experience successes, and we do realize some dreams, there are times and seasons in our lives when we are not so blessed. Life deals us circumstances that keep some of our expectations at bay. There are times in our lives when we feel stuck, making no progress toward our desires. Can anyone relate?

In fact, such times might bring serious frustration. Maybe, we have been so frustrated that we even talked harshly to God about it. We drill God with questions:
- "Why God?"
- "What am I supposed to do?"
- "What do You want from me, God?"
- "Should I be learning a certain lesson?"
- "What's going on here?"
- "Why aren't things working out?"

There is something we want to do, somewhere we want to go, something we feel called by God to accomplish, and yet, that direction cannot be realized for some reason. There is a hindrance. Something is preventing us from progress. Our way is being

Chapter Nine: Foiled by Frustration

blocked. Frustration. It is a pothole that slows many journeys and can prove to be a dead end if allowed.

A friend of mine, Dr. James Littles, suggests that frustration is a gift from God. He thinks that frustration—and the discomfort it causes—enables us to be willing to change, willing to move forward. In other words, he views frustration as one of the means God uses to move us beyond our comfort zone and into something new. There is real merit to this belief.

In order to smooth out frustration's pothole, Psalm 37 contains thoughtful guidance for all who experience this frustration. And more than guidance, these verses contain promise and hope for God's resolution in our lives.

WAYPOINT: **Don't worry.**

In the very opening of this psalm we are instructed not to fret. The New Living Translation reads "Don't worry." Do not fret. We worry about the unknown. We worry about negative possibilities, bad outcomes, or harmful consequences. Certainly, we do not worry about good things happening or about blessings that could

In Case You Were Wandering

happen. No. We worry about the possibility of the bad. For some of us worry happens now and then. For others worry occurs more regularly. For some worry has become a habit. And maybe for some, worry is a lifestyle. But the psalmist reminded us: Don't worry. Stop worrying.

In the Gospels, Jesus spoke of worry also.

"Then He said to His disciples, 'Therefore I say to you, do not worry about your life, what you will eat; nor about the body, what you will put on. Life is more than food, and the body is more than clothing. Consider the ravens, for they neither sow nor reap, which have neither storehouse nor barn; and God feeds them. Of how much more value are you than the birds? And which of you by worrying can add one cubit to his stature? If you then are not able to do the least, why are you anxious for the rest? Consider the lilies, how they grow: they neither toil nor spin; and yet I say to you, even Solomon in all his glory was not arrayed like one of these. If then God so clothes the grass, which today is in the field and tomorrow is thrown into the oven, how much more will He clothe you, O you of little faith? And do not seek what you should eat or what you should drink, nor have an anxious mind. For all these things the nations of the world seek after,

Chapter Nine: **Foiled by Frustration**

and your Father knows that you need these things. But seek the kingdom of God, and all these things shall be added to you'" (Luke 12:22-31).

It is not just the psalmist, but even Jesus told us to stop worrying. He was pretty clear that there is no benefit to worrying. He posed this question, "And which of you by worrying can add one cubit to his stature?" A very revealing question. Worrying does not change things. Think about it. When was the last time you talked to someone who overcame a challenge in their life by worrying about it?

"Hey, I heard you finally found a job. Awesome! How did you find it?"

"Well, I just kept worrying about it and then they called and offered me a job."

"Really? You didn't submit an application? You didn't forward a resume?"

"Nope. I just put on a real good worry."

"And you got the job?"

"Yep. All I had to do was worry."

I have never heard that conversation, and neither have you. Jesus reminds us graphically that worry cannot cause you to grow any taller, and it is not going to change your circumstances. Worrying is not the answer. And believe it or not, the apostle Paul had some thoughts about worrying also. Sure enough, he too was against it.

"Don't worry about anything; instead, pray about everything. Tell God what you need, and thank him for all he has done. Then you will experience God's peace, which exceeds anything we can understand. His peace will guard your hearts and minds as you live in Christ Jesus" (Philippians 4:6-7, NLT).

David, Jesus, and Paul all addressed worrying. They spoke in different times, in different places, to different groups of people and none of them had anything beneficial to say about worrying. Rather, each of them instructed: do not worry. When we are frustrated, we need to hear that command also. Don't worry about it. Pray about it. Then peace will come.

WAYPOINT: Trust in the Lord.

Trust in the Lord. We are commanded to place our faith, belief, hope, confidence, and expectation in Him. Our trust is in the Lord. He is the focus of our expectation. Though it has been written and spoken so many times that it may sound trite, Christians do

Chapter Nine: Foiled by Frustration

not place our trust in houses, in land, in careers, in finance, in circumstances, in talent, in education, in human influence, or power. We do not have to! We place our trust in the Lord. Our trust is in much better hands.

"It is better to trust in the Lord than to put confidence in man. It is better to trust in the Lord than to put confidence in princes" (Psalm 118:8-9).

"Those who trust in the Lord Are like Mount Zion, Which cannot be moved, but abides forever. As the mountains surround Jerusalem, So the Lord surrounds His people from this time forth and forever" (Psalm 125:1-2).

When frustrated, don't worry. Trust in the Lord.

WAYPOINT: **Delight yourself in the Lord.**

Delight speaks of our joy, gladness, and happiness. We are to find our gladness in the Lord. Our joy is founded in Him. He is the center of my happiness. Delight yourself in the Lord.

In Case You Were Wandering

Other psalms speak of delight in the Lord's commands, His ways, His statutes, His testimonies, and His law. But this psalm commands that our delight be in the Lord. Not the various things He has declared, but in the Lord Himself. Our delight is not in the book, but in the Author of the book! More than delighting in the words, we are delighting in the One who gave us the words. We are directed to delight ourselves in Him.

And when we do: "He shall give you the desires of your heart" (Psalm 37:4).

This verse is not a prescription for convincing God to give us the things that we want. Rather, this is a prescription for God to give us the desires we should have. This is necessary because of the human desires that are not in line with our holy God. There are some human desires that will not, and cannot, benefit our spiritual lives. These kinds of desires need to be removed and replaced with desires designed of God Almighty. As we find our satisfaction in God and as we pursue happiness in Him, our human desires fade away and are replaced with godly desires. What an incredible promise. And this replacing of desires could be just the answer for our frustration. When we become frustrated due to an unfulfilled desire, there are two ways to relieve the frustration. We can fulfill the desire, or we can change desires. Delight yourself also in the Lord, and He shall give you the desires of your heart.

Chapter Nine: **Foiled by Frustration**

> **WAYPOINT:** **Commit your way to the Lord.**

Commitment does not seem to be a personal priority in today's culture. In our world, commitment is something sought from others, but not readily offered. And when it is offered, it is not a sure thing. Today's commitment is not what yesterday's commitment was. Commitment now comes with conditions, is now susceptible to circumstance. Commitment was once forever; now it is for a while. Commitment used to keep husbands from leaving their wives and mothers from abandoning their children. That was commitment. An obligation. A pledge. A promise. When the psalmist wrote of this commitment to the Lord, it was not today's commitment, it was the real commitment. No strings attached. No disclaimers. Forever.

We are called to commit our actions and efforts to the Lord. Commit your way to the Lord. We commit our careers to the Lord. We commit our purchases to the Lord. Indeed, we should commit everything we do to the Lord. When we do as we are told, we then receive the promise. And He shall bring it to pass. The promise follows the commitment. God bringing it to pass is based on our willingness to commit it to Him. When frustrated by our future, we relinquish that frustration when we commit our frustrating circumstance to the Lord.

WAYPOINT: **Be still in the Lord.**

I remember special times throughout my life that after the church participated in a special visitation of God's Spirit around an altar, we would not just get up and leave the altar area. Instead, we would sit around the front to stay near the action. We would linger in the presence of God that was evident. I relish the times that while sitting near, remaining prayerful, another wave of God's presence would overcome those who remained close. Be still in the presence of the Lord.

There are times when we quit doing all the talking in prayer, and just be still and allow God to speak, to impact, to minister in our lives. There is a time to stop pouring out all our problems and difficulties before Him and be still in His presence. Resting in the Lord allows His divine nature to impact us personally. We allow Him to calm our fears and frustrations. We allow Him to share with us His perspective, the way He sees things. He helps us to understand that our huge problem is really not all that large in His eyes. Be still

Chapter Nine: **Foiled by Frustration**

in the presence of the Lord and wait patiently for Him. It is a great way to pave over frustration's potholes.

WAYPOINT: **Stop being angry.**

The New Living Translation uses this wording: "Stop being angry! Turn from your rage! Do not lose your temper—it only leads to harm." Here is another one of those things that we are to stop. Stop being angry. While worry typically involves the unknown and the uncertain, anger results from things that have already taken place. Worry is associated with the future; anger is associated with the past. We are angry over a perceived injustice, a perceived wrong. While uncertain why we worry, we are quite certain why we are angry. It is one thing to be told not to worry. It is another thing to be told not to be angry. We are not too certain of the reason for our worry anyway. The focus of our worry is vague. But knowing exactly how we have been wronged justifies our anger. This is not about some vague unknown; we can give you the intricate details for our anger. We can explain it to you clearly. We can give you time, place, action, and culprit. And because we know these details, yielding to "stop being angry" is a bit more difficult than responding to "don't worry." But it is God's command just the same. Stop being angry.

Note also that anger is similar to worry in that it does not produce desired results. In fact, it only leads to harm. Though anger seems justified by the facts, it helps nothing. It only leads to harm. Anger will fuel our frustration rather than relieve it. It is a pothole we need to avoid.

WAYPOINT: **Soon**

"For yet a little while and the wicked shall be no more; Indeed, you will look carefully for his place, But it shall be no more" (Psalm 37:10). When we follow the directives provided in this psalm, soon the thing that has been troubling us will be gone. It shall be no more. What an incredible assurance revealed in this passage. Following Scripture's instructions brings the solution we have desired. Frustration is a pothole we can live without, and the Lord's directives foil frustration before it foils us.

Chapter Ten:

Where Do I Go from Here?

"We give thanks to the God and Father of our Lord Jesus Christ, praying always for you, since we heard of your faith in Christ Jesus and of your love for all the saints; because of the hope which is laid up for you in heaven, of which you heard before in the word of the truth of the gospel, which has come to you, as it has also in all the world, and is bringing forth fruit, as it is also among you since the day you heard and knew the grace of God in truth; as you also learned from Epaphras, our dear fellow servant, who is a faithful minister of Christ on your behalf, who also declared to us your love in the Spirit. For this reason we also, since the day we heard it, do not cease to pray for you, and to ask that you may be filled with the knowledge of His will in all wisdom and spiritual understanding; that you may walk worthy of the Lord, fully pleasing Him, being fruitful in every good work and increasing in the knowledge of God; strengthened with all might, according to His glorious power, for all patience and longsuffering with joy; giving thanks to the Father who has qualified us to be partakers of the inheritance of the saints in the light. He has delivered us from the power of darkness and conveyed us into the kingdom of the Son

In Case You Were Wandering

of His love, in whom we have redemption through His blood, the forgiveness of sins" (Colossians 1:3-14).

The opening to this passage reflects Paul's commendations for the church in Colossae. He began by listing a variety of things that were going good among them. He recognized their faith in Christ Jesus. They already possessed a trust and belief in Christ. Evidently they were committed. Theirs was a public faith that was noticed and spoken of by others. Paul heard of it from someone else. He also heard about their love for all the saints. They were good at taking care of one another. They possessed a genuine concern for each other's needs. They were not selective in their concern. They had love for all of the saints. As our Lord, their love was without respect of persons. Paul went on to reference their hope in Heaven. This group practiced an eternity consciousness. This Heaven-bound focus empowered them to bring forth fruit, to be productive and growing rather than stagnant. Based on Paul's early commendations, this sounds like a really great bunch of people, a solid group of Christians.

I would like to believe that you too have a number of Christian commendations active in your lives. Like Paul, I hope that after spending some time with you, witnessing your life in the kingdom of God, it would be easy to recognize positive aspects of a righteous God being acted out in your day-to-day living. It would be a

Chapter Ten: Where Do I Go from Here?

pleasure to observe and celebrate with you the wonderful works of our loving Savior.

And yet, Paul did not end his discourse with commendations and praises. Instead, he used those as a springboard for his continued prayer for them. Paul added, "For this reason we also... do not cease to pray for you." For this reason. Paul saw their existing virtues as reason to pray further virtues into their lives. Paul was saying, because of your faith, love, and hope, and because of the fruitful work of the gospel in your life, here is what I am praying for you. While recognizing and appreciating the work of the Kingdom that had already taken place in their lives, he still saw greater things in store for them. In his prayer, Paul continued to ask for more. To the great apostle, recognizing God's accomplishments in lives was not an excuse to settle into status quo; instead it was reason to pursue more.

This entire text has been given to practical waypoints that provide directional guidance for our lives. Using them will prove beneficial as you discover the details of the path God has prepared for you. And yet, I feel the need to offer more. I must join with Paul and suggest prayer points to inspire spiritual growth as you proceed along life's path. Waypoints will help you do well. Prayer points will help you excel. As you make use of the waypoints, empower your journey with these prayer points.

In Case You Were Wandering

PRAYER POINT: **Lord, I want to be filled with the knowledge of Your will in all wisdom and spiritual understanding.**

Our prayer, our desire is to know everything that we need to know. That nothing would be left out. Paul's petition was for a clear, complete, and confident picture of God's plan for individual lives. And he prayed that the knowledge of God's will would be in distinct dimensions: wisdom and spiritual understanding. The intent was to understand God's direction on both a natural and a spiritual plane. Further, these two understandings should be in agreement one with the other. Have you ever felt something from God, but it did not make sense in your mind? Or maybe you have reasoned something out in your mind, but simply could not get a peace about it in prayer? Paul prayed that neither of these discrepancies took place. He desired the will of God to be clear in both our natural wisdom and in our spiritual understanding. We should pray for the same.

Chapter Ten: **Where Do I Go from Here?**

PRAYER POINT: **Lord, help me to walk fully pleasing to You.**

Our sinful lives can never be worthy of God's blessing and mercy, yet, we are called to walk within His commands and direction. Paul prayed that these good saints would be fully pleasing to God in their attitudes and actions. He prayed they would have an attitude that desired to please God. Do we follow Christ only when He requires us to do so? Or do we follow Him because we know it makes Him happy? Do we follow His teachings simply because we ought to? Or do we follow His words because we know that when we do, it makes Him smile? The best choice is obvious. What an awesome opportunity we have to make our heavenly Father happy! We should pray for a spirit that seeks to please God.

PRAYER POINT: **Lord, help me to be fruitful in every good work.**

Paul certainly knew how to challenge the church. His prayer went above and beyond those who desired to remain faultless in His sight. This was more than a prayer for prevention; it was a prayer for production. We are not solely called to maintain the person that God has made us, but to grow into more that God would have us to be. Paul prayed, "Be fruitful." Growth, multiplication, and increase are recurring themes in Scripture, particularly in Paul's writing. We cannot be satisfied to say, "Well I'm not what I used to be." Thank the Lord for that. But we must go on to pray, "Lord, what more would you have me to be?"

And while offering this prayer, we are directed to be fruitful in every good work. We are not to leave anything undone. The unwritten message is that we should be careful not to become stagnant in any area of our lives. Mastering a few spiritual disciplines does not excuse us from growing in others. The great prayer warrior must also pursue Bible study. The Bible scholar is called to learn more of fasting. The frequent faster should strengthen his witness. The successful personal evangelist is challenged to practice humility. All are called to be fruitful in every good work. Even the best and brightest have room to grow.

Chapter Ten: **Where Do I Go from Here?**

PRAYER POINT: **Lord, help me to increase in the knowledge of You.**

In our ongoing search for life-direction, and our pursuit of personal growth, no Christian can forget that our fundamental opportunity is to know God. He is pleased with those who desire to understand who He is, what He does, what He purposes, and what He commands. Our desire is to learn the character of God. We want to know the actions of God. Something within us hopes to understand His purposes. Our prayer must be to increase in these things.

But how do we know if we are? Are there specific measurements that signify growth in these areas? In education, we experience regular signs of progress: mid-quarter reports, report cards, diplomas, and degrees. There are definite signs of courses completed. In our careers the same is also true. When we improve there are subsequent signs: pay raises, promotions, and bonus checks. Distinguishing points in knowledge of God are more subtle. In order to recognize them, we can regularly review our spirituality and make notes of positive changes in a journal.

In Case You Were Wandering

We can also invite one of our mentors to help recognize increased spirituality and share those observations. In this way, we can know whether God is answering our prayer to increase our knowledge of Him.

> **PRAYER POINT:** **Lord, strengthen me with Your power for all patience and longsuffering.**

There are times in our lives when we need additional strength that is beyond our own. It is the privilege of Christianity to depend on the glorious power of almighty God to give us added strength. According to the Bible Knowledge Commentary, three words for power are used in this verse. The first one gives us the general thought of being strengthened. The second is translated *power* and refers to "spiritual vitality." The third is translated *might* and refers to "power that overcomes resistance." In other words, Paul recognized that all of this was not going to be easy all of the time. There will be times when we need power that overcomes resistance: resistance of outside forces and resistance from our own human nature. There will be times when we specifically need spiritual vitality so that we can endure with patience. Sometimes deliverance does not arrive as soon as we would like. In those

Chapter Ten: Where Do I Go from Here?

times, we must endure. And we can pray for God's strength to do so with patience.

PRAYER POINT: **Lord, we give You thanks for qualifying, delivering, and redeeming us.**

Paul brought his prayer in this instance to a close with a sure reminder that we must be thankful for the place we have been allowed in the kingdom of God. Truly all of the blessed promises at the fingertips of Christians are due to the incredible grace of God. We are qualified to partake in His inheritance because He desired to qualify us. We are delivered from the power of darkness because He made Himself available to deliver us. We are conveyed into His kingdom because He made a way for us through His death, burial, and resurrection. He provided a means for us to obtain forgiveness for all of our faults when we repent. He made sure we could have all of those faults forever erased through baptism in His name. Then He graciously offers to all His free gift, the Holy Spirit to live within us. Without His interest in us, we would be without any of these undeserved blessings. Surely we must thank Him for these profound things.

In Case You Were Wandering

- ## **My Prayer for You**

As you have invested your money, time, and thoughts into this book, I pray that you have discovered many life-markers to guide you along your path. I pray that you have found inspiration, insight, and resolve. I pray you are no longer a wanderer. I pray you discover the incredible direction that God has prepared for you. Your life is certainly worth it.

Discussion Questions

Session 1 Discussion Questions

1. On a scale of one to ten, one being least sure and ten being most sure, how confident are you in your life-direction? Share some aspects of your life that increase your confidence and some that reduce your confidence.

2. What are some characteristics of our culture that foster aimlessness? What are the forces of culture that encourage you to be a wanderer?

3. Share some of your core values and why you believe they are essential.

4. What do you consider some of the best aspects of your current life-stage? What are some of the most challenging? Can you recognize and explain how these impact your ability to stay true to your life-path?

5. How do the concepts in Psalm 119:33 and Jeremiah 10:23 compare to our culture of independence? While some in our culture feel no need to seek God for life direction, do they seek experts when considering other major decisions? Is this inconsistent? If so, how?

In Case You Were Wandering

Session 2 Discussion Questions

1. Share some recent situations at work or in the classroom where you've needed discernment.

2. Have you ever been accused of being judgmental? Discuss the circumstances surrounding that situation.

3. The video suggests enlisting the guidance of a watchmaker to discern the value of the two pocket watches. Who are the specialists that you seek for counsel in your life, and why?

4. What do you feel are the challenges that make discernment difficult to practice?

5. What can you do on a regular basis to hone your discernment skills?

Session 3 Discussion Questions

1. When trying to convince someone to follow Jesus, what benefits of the kingdom of God do you present, and why?

2. When facing decisions with multiple options, how do you deal with any sense of being overwhelmed?

3. Hyper-spiritual or plainly pragmatic: does one better explain your experience? And if so, explain.

4. If you have taken a personality test, talk about the results. What did you find most insightful from the experience?

5. Share your educational choices and how you made your decisions.

6. In Matthew 26:39-42, it is apparent that Jesus is not very excited about pursuing the Father's will for His life. And yet, He submits His will anyway. If the will of God for your life does not seem exciting, or desirable, how will you respond?

In Case You Were Wandering

Session 4 Discussion Questions

1. If you were Jack or Jill, would you have made any different choices in this relationship? How would you have done so?

2. When discovering differences and commonalities, what sort of activities and discussions provide the best opportunities for you to do so?

3. Due to increasing involvement in online gaming and Internet activity, sociologists recognize the decreasing ability of twentysomething men to engage in social interaction with women. These same sociologists recognize the innate need among twentysomething women for social interaction to initiate and maintain a relationship. Have you witnessed this same issue? Have you been able to overcome the issue, and if so, how?

4. This session talks about the need to find someone going your direction; however, it does not discuss how to find that person. What are the best venues or settings for meeting new people? If you were to create a setting that allowed you to meet new people, how would you do it?

5. Consider a married couple you admire. What characteristics of their relationship do you hope to mimic in your own marriage?

Session 5 Discussion Questions

1. List three people to whom you make yourself personally accountable, and discuss why you chose these individuals.

2. The text offers four questions to ask to enhance your personal accountability. What challenges do you foresee in using these questions regularly?

3. What aspects of time management do you struggle with most, and how have you responded to these struggles?

4. In the last thirty days, what things have brought you frustration? How have you been responding to this frustration?

5. Looking to the next twelve to eighteen months, what are the situations or circumstances that could cause you to battle with worry? Why?

In Case You Were Wandering
Travis Miller

Where are you going right now? Where will you be in twenty years? In five? In one month? How do you answer those big questions like "What am I going to do with my life? Who should I marry? Does God have a plan for me? If so, how do I find it?"

In Case You Were Wandering offers points of reference for young adults to find answers to these questions and others like them. Using practical Christian principles, this book equips twentysomethings to discover purpose in their lives and to stay in pursuit of that purpose.

24709   Small **Group** Package
24707   Book – Paperback
24708   eBook

www.pentecostalpublishing.com